# W.G.GRACE

Bernard Darwin

# W. G. GRACE

with an introduction by John Arlott

**DUCKWORTH**

This edition, with illustrations and introduction, first published 1978
Text, first published 1934, © the Estate of Bernard Darwin
Introduction and editorial arrangement © 1978 by
Gerald Duckworth & Co. Ltd.,
The Old Piano Factory,
43 Gloucester Crescent, London NW1

Book design by
Alphabet and Image, Sherborne, Dorset

*The illustration on page 1 is of a bronze statuette of W. G. Grace,*
*and the portrait on page 2 is an oil painting by J. Ernest Breun 1895.*

ISBN: 0 7156 1037 6

Filmset and printed in Great Britain by
BAS Printers Limited, Over Wallop, Hampshire

# CONTENTS

# INTRODUCTION

There are over a dozen books about W. G. Grace, including at least eight biographies and an autobiography. Others have been larger than this, have ranged in greater detail over his performances. None, though, has shown greater understanding or appreciation of him as both a person and a player than this life which the author once described as 'only a very little one'.

Its distinction, like that of all the best books on sporting subjects, lies in the fact that it is not simply a sports book but a universally valid book on a sporting subject. Primarily as golf correspondent of *The Times*, but also as an essayist and biographer on cricket and boxing, Bernard Darwin was one of the first to lift sports writing beyond the parochial limits of its subject and make it acceptable to readers outside its strict following. In the simultaneously nostalgic and imaginatively and hungry British society of the period immediately after the First World War, he and Neville Cardus, in their contrasting fashions, wrote to a standard of literacy the sports pages of the press had never known before. They were essentially different in style; Neville Cardus in his later years declared himself embarrassed by the 'greenery yallery' extravagances of his youth. Bernard Darwin, perhaps from his early legal training, had a cooler approach: he was at pains never to over-write, even if the effort sometimes took him in the opposite direction. The two are, however, complementary figures and their joint effect has coloured and shaped all informed British sports writing since their day.

Darwin illuminated golf because although he understood the technique of the game well, he was concerned with humanity, its humour as well as its humours. Like a number of the writers of his period, too – including Cardus and the similarly literate football reporter, H. D. Davies ('Old International') – he had a deep appreciation and wide knowledge of Charles Dickens.

Born in 1876, Bernard Darwin was the grandson of the author of *Origin of Species*, whom he dimly recollected from childhood when he 'had no notion that he was of any save domestic consideration'. He went to Eton where his enthusiasm for cricket 'soon dwindled feebly away under a certain lack of encouragement' and on to Cambridge where for three years he played golf for the University, as captain in the third. Called to the Bar in 1903, he practised briefly in 'no more than a flirtation with the law'; golf proved compulsive.

From 1907 he contributed articles called 'Tee Shots' to *The Evening Standard* and occasional essays to *The Times* and *Country Life*. He had, though, no journalistic training or background – he took to writing as by second nature and the period of his eminence began, contemporaneously with that of Cardus, in 1919 as soon as he joined the staff of *The Times*. He remained there, as golf correspondent, until 1954; and contributed occasional essays in his retirement. It is an important aspect of his eminence that he never allowed himself to be confined by the subject on which he was outstandingly expert.

His books include *Present Day Golf* (with George Duncan, 1921), *Golf Between Two Wars*, *Golf Courses of Great Britain*, essays in golf appreciation like *Tee Shots and Others*, *Playing the Like* and *Out of the Rough*; reminiscences in *Life is Sweet, Brother*, *Green Memories*, and *Pack Clouds Away*, which contain some felicitous writings on cricket; but also *John Gully and His Times*, about the early nineteenth century boxer and his social background; *The Game's Afoot*, an anthology of sports writing; *The English Public School*; and three books on Dickens.

As a golfer he was good enough to reach the semi-final of the Amateur Championship on two occasions, to win the Golf Illustrated Gold Vase, the President's Putter and, with Miss Joyce Wethered, the Worplesdon Foursomes; and he played in eight international matches against Scotland. The high point of his career, however, came in 1922 when he was *The Times* correspondent with the British team in the United States. The captain fell ill, and Darwin was invited to play in his place: he did so – and reported the match as well.

His standing in the game was high, not simply as one who had played it well – others had done that better – but as one who had presented it to the public in a more objective, accurate and attractive way than anyone else had ever done. Hence he was honoured with the captaincy of the Royal and Ancient Club, made captain and then President of the Oxford and Cambridge Golfing Society: in 1937 he was awarded the C.B.E. From his first, irregular contributions until his retirement, his work for *The Times* spanned forty-six years and his farewell dinner was attended by golfers from all walks of life.

Bernard Darwin was one of the few great writers on sport, a man of style, perception, clarity; of wit which could be pointed but which was, in tune with his nature, essentially kind. He had a profound memory for events, feelings and facts; an immense integrity and fidelity; a gift for conversation but, as one sensitive to bores, he never bored. His wife, née Elinor Mary Monsell, collaborated in, and illustrated, some of his books of light verse. They had one son – the painter, Robin Darwin – and two daughters. Bernard Darwin died in 1960.

Some years after he wrote this life of Grace Darwin twice returned to the subject in other essays. He begins 'Some Towering Shades' with:

> One winter morning about 1910 Mr. Riddell's car pulled up outside my small house in Chelsea to take me to play golf at Walton Heath. Inside it I discerned the massive figure of Dr. W. G. Grace. He kissed his hand very prettily to my small daughter, flattening her nose against the window pane, and said to me, when I was introduced to him, 'You're rather like my son the Commander.'
>
> That was a day to be marked with a white stone, for to any hero-worshipper in the field of sport, the first time of meeting W.G. was unlike that of meeting anybody else. There have been other heroes but he towers high over them all. His fame is of a different quality to theirs; many of them will live, if at all, only as figures in the W.G. legend; he was, as Tom Emmett said, 'a non-such'.

At another point he observes, 'The three qualities that struck me particularly in W.G. were his dignity, his modesty and his

*Bernard Darwin*

boyishness.' He could only have written this book, or any other, as he felt and believed it and there is a key to him as both man and writer in the passage:

> So my task was not an easy one, and I have always been dreadfully sorry because I am afraid I hurt his son, the late Vice-Admiral Edgar Grace, the 'Commander' whom I was supposed to resemble. He was most kind to me; he asked me to stay with him and told me many interesting and pleasant things about his father's life at home. When I sent him a copy of the little book, not without trepidation, he said that he was grateful for the affectionate way I had written of his father but that I 'had made too many excuses for him'. Of course I felt guilty, though in looking back I do not think I had any real reason. It would have been absurd to write of W.G. as the perfect example of the *preux chevalier*, and that is what he clearly was to the son. I remember particularly his saying how splendid his father used to look in his dress clothes, with a vast expanse of gleaming shirt front on the few occasions when he and Mrs Grace went out to dinner and the children saw them off at the front door. It would have been impossible to satisfy that touching and complete admiration. I am very unlikely ever to be asked to write anybody else's life, but, if I were, I do not think I would attempt it should any of his children be alive. The risk of hurt feelings is scarcely worth the running.

Seven years later he returned to the same theme, quoted the Admiral's comment and continued:

> I will not fall into the same error again. No doubt he [W.G.] had his faults but they came from his intense keenness on the game, and those who knew him best not merely condoned them but loved him, I think, almost better for them. He had a wonderful power of inspiring affection, and to know him ever so slightly was to understand and to fall under the spell. When my eldest daughter was two years old W.G. kissed his hand to her in the prettiest way, as she gazed at him through the window. I have always impressed on her that if she lives to a hundred she can never have paid to her a pleasanter honour.

*John Arlott*

'Had Grace been born in Ancient Greece, the Iliad would have been
a different book.' JOHN PERCEVAL, BISHOP OF HEREFORD

# FOREWORD

I MUST begin this small book by saying that I have not attempted any technical appraising of W. G. as a cricketer. It would be an impertinence for one so ill equipped to do so, and in any case it has been done over and over again by those who have the right and the knowledge. Mr. C. E. Green's words, 'The greatest cricketer that ever lived or ever will live,' are good enough for me.

Neither have I set out what W. G. did in any statistical form*; I have mentioned his averages, if at all, incidentally. All I have attempted as regards his cricket is to give, of necessity very briefly, a summary of his achievements season by season during his long career. In doing so I have borrowed freely from other people's books, in particular from Mr. H. S. Altham's *History of Cricket*, from three of W. G.'s own works, *Cricket, W.G.*, and *The History of a Hundred Centuries*, and from the *Memorial Biography*. That book upon which Sir Home Gordon spent so much time and trouble, is a repository of W. G. stories, and some of these I have stolen, but I have tried to do so sparingly, since many of them are by this time very well known. Moreover they need telling with a Gloucestershire accent. Alas that Arthur Croome is no longer here to tell them, or in default of that to write them.

*A brief statistical summary of W. G. Grace's career, with additional notes, has been prepared by G. Neville Weston and appears on pages 121-4.

W. G.'s life was divided by a sharp line into two parts. As a cricketer he was the best known public figure in England. As a private citizen he was an ordinary mortal, and a very modest one, who did not think that people would be interested in his private affairs. Except for some account of his boyhood at Downend, he said nothing in his writings about his everyday life, and very little has been said of it elsewhere. That blank I have endeavoured in a very small way to fill, and here I must most gratefully acknowledge the help of Vice-Admiral H. E. Grace, W. G.'s eldest surviving son, who has told me a number of things which I could not otherwise have known, and given me the pleasantest insight into a very pleasant family life. It is hard for me to thank him enough for his kindness and friendliness.

Not only did I bother Admiral Grace, but also several distinguished cricketers of my acquaintance who played with W. G. They all did their best for me, most readily and patiently, and I must especially mention Mr. A. J. Webbe, Sir Stanley Jackson, Mr. George Brann, Mr. Gilbert Jessop, Mr. H. D. G. Leveson-Gower, and Mr. C. M. Wells. Indeed I should have liked to spend my life in plaguing these and other eminent persons, and making them talk about W. G. for ever. Only considerations of time and space have saved me from temptation and them from a grievous infliction.

I had myself the great privilege of meeting W. G. in the later years of his life, and the great fun of playing some games of golf with him. I can say at least that I knew him well enough to understand the deep affection of all his friends. Anybody who talks to cricketers about him must be struck as much by their devotion to him as a man as by their reverence for him as a supreme player. If in what follows that point is not made clear, then the fault is wholly that of the writer and not of those who tried to help him.

B. D.

IN the year 1934, the roar of the Test Matches in Australia had only just died away. How much of all that hub-bub was due to an inconsiderable domestic event that happened a hundred and three years before, and may perhaps have been given a third of a column in a local paper?

It was in the year 1831 that a young doctor, Henry Mills Grace by name, married Miss Martha Pocock, and settled down to a country practice in the small Gloucestershire village of Downend near Bristol. Gloucester be it observed and not Somerset, although Dr. Grace had been born over the border at Long Ashton. Had he stayed in his native place the history of cricket as a British institution, which he was to affect beyond all computation, might not have been changed, but the story of county cricket would have been altogether different. Francis Thompson would have written:

> *It is Somerset coming north, the irresistible*
> *The shire of the Graces long ago.*

That young man who was destined through his offspring to change the face of England had chosen his wife well for the purpose, for it was said of her by Richard Daft that she 'knew ten times as much about cricket as any lady he ever knew.' She was the daughter of Mr. George Pocock, who kept what was then the most

popular and successful school in Bristol. He had another and more singular claim to celebrity, in that he invented a carriage to be drawn by a kite. What is more, he successfully drove it – if that be the right term – to London. Roads that wound excessively through villages were troublesome, and chimneypots were occasionally knocked off, as his grandson in after years rejoiced to tell. Still he made the journey to London, and is said to have exhibited his carriage to George IV. We know Mrs. Grace, in pictures, as a handsome middle-aged lady in ringlets. In one of them she is standing, consciously still, by a table bearing a flower-pot, and were she but to move a muscle we could hear the rustling of her best silk gown. She has large features, an expression at once very kindly and a little formidable, and an eye to threaten and command anyone not doing his duty in the field. In another she is playing the harp. She looks well fitted to be a mother of men, and for nearly twenty years at steady intervals her family grew. The eldest son Henry was born in 1833, Alfred in 1840, Edward Mills in 1841, William Gilbert on July 18th, 1848, George Frederick in 1850. There were also four daughters, trifling by comparison, who arrived at various times not generally deemed worthy of more precise record, between Henry and William Gilbert.

To support so large a family a village doctor must work hard,

*wnend House, Grace's birthplace*

*The room in which W.G. was born*

and Dr. Grace rode early and late to see his many patients in a large straggling practice. Still he managed to make time for a little hunting with the Duke of Beaufort's in winter, and for a little cricket in summer. He had always been fond of the game, and, though no more than a fair player, had, in his medical student days, played now and then between five and eight o'clock in the morning on Durdham Down. For a while he could do no more than dash into Clifton to watch a match for an hour or two, but as soon as the eldest of his boys was big enough to hold a bat he seized the opportunity to make a pitch in the garden. It is pleasant to think that he did so not wholly for the boy's sake but because, as is always the way with the best of grown-up players with children, he longed to play himself.

It was, then, about 1841 that the doctor and the young Henry began to play together in front of Downend House. The next in order were but ineffectual girls, and so we may leave this manly game of single wicket for a moment and survey the game in the greater world outside Downend as it was in this memorable year. The old Hambledon era was definitely past and gone. 'The remains of the once great, glorious, and unrivalled William Beldham' still survived; indeed he was a hearty old man of seventy, working in his garden at eight o'clock in the morning, destined to

GRAND CRICKET MATCH, AT BRIGHTON.

live for another twenty years, so that W. G. himself might, as a boy, have seen him and kissed his bat even as did the Reverend Mr. Mitford. Lambert, long since warned off Lord's Ground for roguery, was even now making runs in local Surrey cricket, though over sixty. Osbaldeston, still a great man on a horse, had ceased to devastate the country with his fast bowling. The Rev. Lord Frederick Beauclerk, something well over sixty now, watched and ruled at Lord's a martinet, but the happy days when he had counted on cricket for £600 a year were over. After these great ones there had been a time of lesser men, but now an heroic age had come again, for the 'forties were the days of Fuller Pilch and Alfred Mynn:

> *When the grand old Kent eleven full of pluck and hope began*
> *That great battle with All England single-handed man to man.*

Not even Hampshire at its zenith had enjoyed a fame more splendid than was now Kent's, but it was still a fame spread only over parts of England. Cricket was for the most part a southern game. There was Nottingham to be sure, always a breeder of cricketers: Old Clarke was at his best, though not yet recognised, and Redgate in his brief prime was a great bowler, but Jackson, Tinley, and the rest were to come, and Lancashire was hardly born as a cricketing county. Yorkshire had Sheffield – but what was Sheffield as compared with Bearsted and Town Malling? One of its champions, Marsden, had tried some years before to play Fuller Pilch at single wicket, and had been smashed like an eggshell. Then a dauntless little man called Dearman had shown 'unflinching bottom' but very little wisdom in challenging Alfred Mynn. The

*Fuller Pilch*

good-natured Goliath had given him a few balls to hit, but presently the crowd had shouted, 'Finish him off, Alfred,' and his middle stump had been sent spinning like a catherine-wheel by the *coup de grace*. The west was in far deeper darkness than the north; it had produced no cricketer ever heard of at Lord's and the Oval. Clarke, the great missionary of cricket, had not begun to spread the gospel with his touring team of all the talents. No rustic champion had yet come home to the village green, black-eyed and arm in sling, to say proudly, 'I had a hover of Jackson.'

Amateur cricket generally was in a poor way, since in this very year, 1841, the M.C.C. refused to organise the match between Gentlemen and Players. True the tide was just about to be turned by the Kentish giant Alfred Mynn, just as some twenty years later it was to be turned by another giant from Gloucestershire, but at the moment the Gentlemen were at once lazy and despondent. Public-school cricketers had not yet begun to be coached, and the game was as casual at schools as we see it depicted in *Tom Brown's Schooldays*. A young public-school or university player would have been glad enough to play for his county, but, if his county were one of three or four great ones, he was seldom good enough, and, says Mr. Charles Box proudly, 'not the wealth of the Indies or the interest of both Houses of Parliament put together would have gained him admission into the county ranks, unless he could pass muster with the experienced hands who had charge of the regiment.' Generally speaking it was the amateur's part – and an amateur then simply meant a gentleman – to find the money, and to back his side rather than to play for it.

Finally, cricket had a few years before passed through a momentous legislative crisis. Lillywhite and Broadbridge had for years been defying the laws of bowling with the connivance of the umpires, and doubtless others had followed their example. At last the M.C.C. had taken action, their hand forced, perhaps, as it was to be forced nearly thirty years later by that other intrepid Lillywhite who no-balled Edgar Willsher; they allowed the bowler's hand to be raised to the height of the shoulder. Poor Mr. Willes of early round-arm fame, who had galloped out of Lord's in a pet and galloped out of cricket for ever, had been retrospectively canonised.

Such, very briefly, was the world of cricket into which the eldest of the Graces was being introduced by his father, but it was, as has been said, a world with very definite and narrow boundaries, and Gloucester and Somerset were as yet hardly within them. There

*Alfred Mynn*

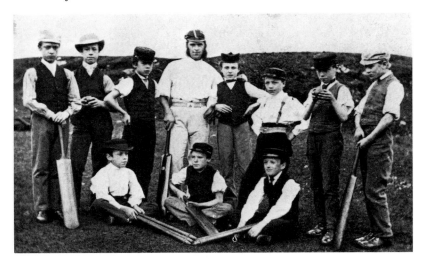

*A young XI on Clifton Downs in the middle of the nineteenth century*

were four or five clubs in the neighbourhood of Bristol, one of them sixteen years old, but that was all. The fuel must have been there only waiting for a spark, for as soon as Dr. Grace made his pitch the neighbours began to take an interest, and in the next three or four years the Mangotsfield club was founded, with Rodway Hill as its ground, and the Doctor as its acknowledged leader.

He had definite and serious views about the game, writing out his team a week beforehand in his note-book; marking his two bowlers, his two change bowlers and – a most important person – his longstop. He insisted on good fielding, and had strength of character enough to make his neighbours come to fielding practice in the evenings. He was a patient batsman, not to be tempted into hitting unless he had a mind to it, and a steady left-hand bowler; further, he possessed a quality in which his sons were never deficient – a resolution to stick up for his rights. There is one story in which he appears positively alarming. A match was made for a stake, and the Doctor did not wholly approve of that to begin with, the more so, perhaps, as it was a match apparently foredoomed to be lost. On the appointed day the captain of the other side chaffingly insisted on the stake being posted: the Doctor and his men gravely produced their money, and then, where was the other side's? They had either been too sure of victory or they had forgotten to bring it. There was a formidable outburst. We can see the Doctor rating the Bristol men as soundly as they doubtless deserved. Did he say, as his son did many years afterwards, 'Won't have it, can't have it, and shan't have it'? At any rate he made them hand over their gold

*The Chestnuts, Downend, Bristol, to which the Grace family moved in 1850*

watches to make up the stake before the match proceeded; then, largely by his own stone-walling and accurate bowling (there was someone bowling fast sneaks at the other end), he brought off an astounding victory. It was a long time, we are told, before the losers heard the last of that match. If the father was like the son, we may feel tolerably sure that this is not overstating the case.

In that match, there took part – on the wrong side – another member of the family, Alfred Pocock, who was, in a minor capacity, to help found its fortunes. Uncle Pocock (he sounds as if he came out of a George Eliot novel) lived in Bristol. He had apparently played little cricket as a boy, but he was fired by his brother-in-law's example, and was a natural ball-game player. He worked hard at the game in his spare moments, was an earnest student of its theory and enthusiastic enough about its practice to walk twelve miles, from Bristol to Downend and back. Evidently he had that genuine passion for the game which goes far beyond a mere personal enjoyment of it, and his coaching was to be invaluable to his nephews as one after the other they attained the earliest possible age for batting without tears.

There were two other members of the family who helped the Mangotsfield fortunes – two young cousins, William Rees and George Gilbert, who spent their holidays at Downend. Gradually the rival club, the West Gloucestershire, was subdued. Of this club the members consisted of young men from the universities, who came to be coached by a local parson, and sometimes there were among them competent cricketers, but *How should it stand before all resistless Graces?* In 1846 the weaker party agreed to amalgamation, and was consoled by its title being chosen for the new club: the conquering Mangotsfield was born again under the name of the conquered West Gloucestershire. One of its first matches was that of which the infant W.G. (he was called Gilbert by his family) used to be told as soon as he was old enough to be told anything. In place of fabulous giants and ogres, he heard about the great Mr. Marcon who had once been seen on Rodway Hill. 'Mr. Marcon,' so ran the terrific legend, 'did not trouble about the length of the ball. He aimed at the wicket, and the ball flew straight from his hand to it without touching the ground; and nearly every time it hit the bottom of the stump, the stump was smashed.' Half the side never saw the ball; one man had tried to plant his bat firmly in the block, and the bat had been driven clean through the wicket. No doubt the story grew ever the more awful in the telling, so that a more imaginative little boy might have dreamed of Mr. Marcon and woken raving: he might have suspected Mr. Marcon in every shadowy corner of the house, and felt the invisible rush of him coming nearer and nearer down the dark passage.

It was in 1846 that Mr. Marcon had come down like the wolf on the Mangotsfield fold; two years later W. G. was born, and in that same year Henry, now fifteen years old, played his first match for the club. Two years later again, in 1850, the family, having outgrown Downend House, moved over the way to the Chestnuts, and Dr. Grace at once set to work to cut down some of the apple-trees in the orchard and make a pitch. It was small to begin with, but grew larger as the boys grew up, and by the time W. G. was old enough to understand such things it was, he says, 'worthy of a first-class club.' Henry was now beginning to learn the family business of medicine, and incidentally he learned it well, for W. G. was later known to say, casting something of a covert slur on the rest of the family, 'My brother Henry, he was a good doctor, he was.' Father and son went on their rounds together, but made time for half an hour's cricket on the family pitch after luncheon, and E. M. was now, of course, old enough – he was ten in 1851 – to begin the more serious occupation of life.

# 2

# 1854-1865

THE pitch was ready in 1851, and in 1854 the small W. G., who had gone his earliest walks round it as another child walks round the garden, was ready to play there. This was the earliest summer that he could remember, and, apart from his own cricket, there was one great event in it, the coming of Clarke's All-England Eleven to Bristol, to play against a local twenty-two led by Dr. Grace. The boy had been with his father to see the ground being made ready, and now he went to the match with his mother, who sat watching it all day long in her pony chaise. He did not remember much about it afterwards, except that some of the All-England men played in tall hats, but luckily Mrs. Grace kept a series of scrap-books into which she pasted cuttings and scores; so that we know the names of the funny tall-hatted gentlemen – George Parr and Caffyn and Willsher, Clarke and Bickley and Box, and one that must have been confusing to the infant mind, if it had begun the history of England, Julius Caesar. The invaders came again in the next year, and this time not only did the Doctor, Uncle Pocock, Henry, and Alfred play for the twenty-two, but E. M., now fourteen years old, was specially sent for from his school at Long Ashton. He was given out l.b.w., an event seldom regarded with complete equanimity by any member of the family, but he had something to console him: that kind old Mr. Clarke gave him a bat for his good longstopping, and he hung it up, like a trophy, on his mother's pony chaise. Neither was Mrs. Grace forgotten. She had a book on cricket, with a solemn inscription, 'Presented to Mrs. Grace by William Clarke, Secretary, All-England Eleven.' The twenty-two were crushed again, chiefly by Bickley's bowling, but there was the bat and the book – nothing could take them away.

Meanwhile the course of study was being steadily pursued in the orchard. The pitch was open for play in March and closed in October, but there was cricket of sorts all the year round, sometimes with a wicket chalked on a wall and a good-natured stable-boy for bowler. The family practices were conducted under strict rules, a quarter of an hour's innings for the grown-ups and five minutes for the small ones, who had to take it out in fielding. As E. M. was now a big strong boy with a natural pull, and there was a wood and a quarry in the direction of long on, the fielding was in the nature of salvage work. Mrs. Grace and the girls looked on, and threw up a ball if it was hit near them, and occasionally bowled, but only to the very small. There were three fielders, however, whose names must never be forgotten, an immortal trinity in the history of cricket, Don, Ponto, and Noble. They were particularly useful when the ball was hit into woods or water, but they did not only field out in the deep. All three were prepared to stop the hardest hit with their chests, and were not afraid of a catch. As in one of the Robin Hood ballads:

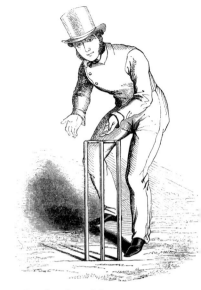

*Box keeping wicket*

> *The curtal dogs so taught they were*
> *They caught the arrowes in their mouth.*

Ponto, in particular, had views on the game and the direction in which a ball should be hit. His place was by the bowler, and he strongly reprobated E. M.'s pull.

This gorgeous heterodoxy of E. M.'s was believed to be due to his playing too early in life with a full-sized bat. It is not known now whose fault it was, but it is my own belief that Uncle Pocock thought it was the Doctor's fault, that he had urged and begged that the boy should not have too big a bat, and that the Doctor had brushed his remonstrances aside. Thereupon Uncle Pocock took a great fancy for coaching the small W. G., making himself his especial servant, resolving in his own heart that his particular boy should eclipse E. M., and that thus he, Uncle Pocock, should be even with his brother-in-law. There is no authority whatever for this legend, but I insist on believing in it. At any rate, Uncle Pocock did coach the boy with unwearying patience, making him use a

*E. M. Grace 1863*

small bat, and giving him as his highest ambition to play straight and keep the ball out of the wicket. As Harry Hall, the gingerbread baker of Farnham, had drummed into William Beldham the doctrine of the left elbow up, so, now, Uncle Pocock exhorted over and over again, 'Keep your left shoulder well forward, and get over the ball.' The ball must be watched intently: there was to be no wild hitting, nothing which would evoke from Ponto a censorious growl. Patience, defence, a straight bat – those were the things that really mattered, the things worth living and dying for; and the pupil saw that the master was right, and strove to be worthy. 'All is vanity but cricket,' had exclaimed the Reverend Mr. Mitford some twenty years before, in bidding farewell to the Hambledon eleven. There was arising in that Gloucestershire orchard a greater than any of the Hampshire men, and he held fast to Mr. Mitford's view.

This work of drilling, so patient on both sides, soon began to bear fruit. By the time he was nine years old the small boy was beginning to be a tall strong boy for his age. He had been seriously ill with pneumonia and grew all the faster after it. He could do something more than ward off his uncle's attack; he could, as he says, 'play a ball from his wicket with a fair amount of confidence.' By the time he was ten he had the unspeakable honour of playing for the West Gloucestershire Club, but his scores were not then, or for a year or two later, very large. The cousin, William Rees, who had been one of the early champions of Mangotsfield, came back after a six years absence to play for the club. He was W. G.'s godfather; perhaps he had forgotten to give him a christening mug; at any rate he now thought so well of him that he gave him a bat, and one with a cane handle: not even E. M.'s bat from the great Clarke had been more glorious. Two years later, in 1860, just before his twelfth birthday, the boy made 51 with that bat against Clifton, 35 not out on the first day – 'very patiently and correctly, they say,' – and 16 more the next morning. 'I do not think,' he says, in retrospect, 'that my greatest efforts have given me more pleasure than that first big innings.' The family standard was high, for E. M. was verging on greatness even then; discipline was maintained, and there was no spoiling of an infant phenomenon; moreover there was Fred, now ten years old, and showing extraordinary promise: but the father and mother allowed themselves this time to be a little proud.

The next year there came something of a setback, under 50 runs for ten innings; nor did anything epoch-making happen in 1862, but there was cricket all the time – hard toil both at batting and bowling, cricket at Downend, cricket for other local clubs besides West Gloucestershire, and cricket at school. School does not play a very large part in the Grace's history. E. M. went to Kempe's School at Long Ashton, where, on one occasion, he appears to have shown signs of future greatness. On being unanimously given out l.b.w. by all the players, he went out, but carried the stumps away with him. W. G. went first to a dame's school close to his home, kept by an agreeable old lady called Miss Trotman, then to two other private schools in the neighbourhood. He was also coached by a clergyman, Mr. Dann, who afterwards married his sister Blanche, and so became his brother-in-law. Whatever he learned, it is tolerably certain that he looked over the edge of his lessons for his cricket to begin. Henry had now married and set up for himself: he was captain of a club at Hanham (the birthplace of the great Tom Cribb), and used to ask his young brother to play for him. Sometimes there were family battles: E. M. once played for Bitton against Hanham, and in the end Bitton went in to get ten runs to win. E. M. said he would make them in one hit, and was bowled first ball; wicket after wicket fell, the Bittonians, who had got out of their flannels, had to come in to bat in their workaday clothes. A solitary batsman made three, and three were run for a bye. Henry and W. G. got all the wickets between them. Hanham won by three runs, and there was another addition to those family jokes which the defeated parties were not allowed to forget.

That match, however, did not take place till 1864, and we are anticipating a little. Up to 1863, W. G. was steadily making a local reputation. In that year he made a distinct step forward when he played for the first time against professional bowling of the highest class. The All-England Eleven came down to play twenty-two of Bristol on Durdham Down. There were still some of the great ones, dimly remembered in tall hats from nine years before – Stephenson, Willsher, Caesar, and Anderson; there were also formidable reinforcements, Hayward, Tarrant, and Jackson, and of those last two mighty fast bowlers it must be remembered that W. G. maintained in after life that he had never played against any better, unless it was George Freeman. Tarrant good-naturedly bowled to the boy for ten minutes in the luncheon interval; E. M. had played for the All-England Eleven, and they had probably a kindly feeling towards his young brother. Tarrant and Jackson were bowling when W. G. came in, and, though he says he felt very anxious, he soon began to score freely. There came Tinley with insidous lobs. The boy watched him carefully for an over, and then

*Stephenson and Caffyn. Their clothes seem strange even for nineteenth century cricketers, and perhaps reflect their pioneering spirit : both men had been on the first tour to America in 1859, and the first tour to Australia in 1862–3. E. M. Grace accompanied Caffyn to Australia the next year.*

hit him into the tent for six. Perhaps he said truculently to himself, as he said aloud many years afterwards, 'I rather like these bowlers that break both ways – to the boundary.' At any rate he jumped out to hit another six and was bowled. Still, he had made 32 runs, at fifteen years old, against the best bowling in England. Was not that to strike the stars?

Already those who had eyes to see must have known that here was a portent. One person at any rate had known it for some time. Mrs. Grace had written to George Parr asking him to give E. M. a place in the All-England Eleven. She said modestly that he had the makings of a fine player. She added that she had another boy growing up who would be a better batsman than any of his brothers, for his back play was sounder than theirs. Let us hope she showed Uncle Pocock the letter before she posted it.

His mother had been too humble about E. M., for since he had been twenty-one he had been flogging the hearts out of all the bowlers he met. In the west country he spread such terror that it was solemnly proposed that he should not be allowed to play, and perhaps W. G. never had so great a compliment paid to him as this, no, not even when later on Tom Emmett said he ought to be made to play 'with a littler bat.' In 1862, E. M. had burst like a rude thunderbolt into the tranquil blue sky of the Canterbury Week. It was suggested that he should be sent for, as one side were a man short. His father, who was staying at Canterbury, said that it was not worth his coming all that way for half a match unless he could also play for the M.C.C., of which he was not then a member, against the Gentlemen of Kent. The Kent secretary gave in and promised. The Gentlemen of Kent must have heard a good deal about E. M., for, with a premonition of what was to come, they protested. Their foreboding was amply justified, for the substitute carried his bat through for 192, and took all ten wickets in the Kent second innings.

In that year, E. M. had an average of 40 for forty innings, as compared with the 31 of Carpenter and the 22 of Daft. It is true that a good many of his matches were not first class, though the distinction in those days was hardly a clearcut one. However, in 1863 he played for the All-England Eleven, for North and South, and for Gentlemen *v.* Players, and his average was 35 for twenty-seven innings against Daft's 34 for nine innings. In fact he was the most prolific, and by far the most alarming, run-getter of his day, with a nerve that rose joyfully to the occasion, and a unique power of treating the best of bowlers as if, in a happy phrase of Mr. R. H. Lyttleton's about another great hitter, they were charity school-boys. Not only that, but he was an excellent round-arm bowler, liable to break into lobs without the formality of a warning, and as quick as lightning in the field, '*the* best point,' in the words of Richard Daft, 'that has yet been seen.'

So tremendous a player must at any time make a stir in the world of cricket, but the stir that E. M. made was all the greater because of the scandalous manner in which he outraged every law of batting that had hitherto been held sacred. Men shouted involuntarily with joy at his hitting, and then growled to themselves that it was not cricket. The world's view was that of the sagacious Ponto, that a ball on the off must be played to the off, and here was a young man who deliberately picked the good length ball just outside the off stump to be slashed with a cross bat to long-on. It was indecent, and it horrified Mr. Pycroft. That delightful writer played in his later cricketing years in Somersetshire, and, speaking of his very last match, he said to Mr. Bettesworth, 'I remember that I went in third and that Teddy Grace was at the other end.' The poor old gentleman made 40 runs, but he had palpitations of the heart, enhanced perhaps by having to run out his young partner's disgraceful hits. That was in 1860, when E. M. was only on the threshold. Three years later he had risen to such heights that he

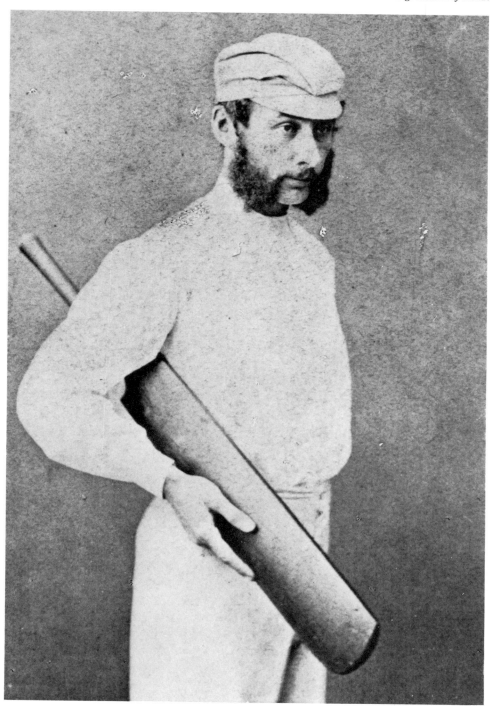

*1. Grace in the 1860s :*
*spread terror wherever*
*he went*

could not be passed over in disapproving silence. Mr. Pycroft reprobated his methods, and then, yielding to the evidence of scores, tried to prove that his unorthodoxy was partly an optical illusion. Finally he gave it up in despair, and admitted that E. M. might say, 'If my style is not counted good play, it is high time it were.'

That innings of the young W. G.'s against three such bowlers was not forgotten, and next year, in 1864, though he was not quite sixteen, he was asked to play for the All-England Eleven against an eighteen of Lansdown. Since Lansdown had not snapped him up, he was proud and glad to accept. E. M., who had gone to Australia with George Parr's team, had stayed there longer than the others, and was not yet at home: the boy alone carried the family honour on his shoulders for All-England, while Henry took his place humbly on the side of the eighteen.

Old Clarke had retired by now, and All-England were led by George Parr the 'Lion of the North.' This Eleven was not the only one in the field, for some years before there had been a schism. Clarke, something too dictatorial as captain, and something too 'near' as to money, had quarrelled with some of his men, and the seceders had formed the United All-England Eleven. There were, however, enough good players to go round, and the greater glory still belonged to the original team. It must have been an odd life that they led, with something of the humours and discomforts, the anxieties about the money and the lodgings and the gate, the jokes and the quarrels and the journeys, of a small theatrical company. They have been well described by Richard Daft, and we can still see them, in their habit as they lived, in faded old photographs, with their whiskers and their Newgate fringes, their shirts of red and white spots, the All-England colours, their small billycocks perching uneasily on their heads, their bow-ties and their belts, their sagging white trousers and their brown boots. How hard it is today to believe that any man in whiskers was ever a great player of games. Even with W. G. before us, and Blackham and Bonner and other of the early Australians, beards test our faith, and whiskers appear more prohibitive of skill even than the bowler-hats. George Parr looks, in the words of the Alfred Mynn elegy, 'like a king among them all,' handsome and dignified. The others have a beery, rustic, village-green air. And yet they were mighty cricketers, and, especially, mighty fast bowlers, giants who spread death and destruction through all the pigmy ranks they encountered from Northumberland to Cornwall.

*George Parr :*
*Lion of the North*

For one professional to manage an eleven of professionals has never been an easy task, and this cannot have been an easy team for George Parr to drive. Fortunately he was something above most of them in social position, and to be 'a better gentleman' is always a valuable asset. He grew irritated with them sometimes, for he seems to have been a singular, highly strung man, full of contradictory little ways. He was afraid of no fast bowler on any wicket, but was afraid of being drowned whenever he went on the sea; he clutched his old hat-box like a nervous old lady afraid of pickpockets, and scowled at the most innocent porter who wanted to carry it; he locked himself in a cellar if he thought there might be thunder; he looked sadly at his tongue in the morning when he thought he had smoked one cigar too many the night before. He was sure that the boots at the inn was a villain and would steal the funds; he was worried to death lest that wild John Jackson should get into some absurd scrape and have to be left behind or bailed out. Perhaps he was half amused all the time at his own anxieties, and he seems to have managed his queer team by giving them all nicknames; Jackson was the Fog Horn, because he blew his nose with so triumphant a note whenever he bowled down a wicket; Tinley was the Spider, Anderson was the Old Scotchman, and Tarrant was Tear'em – ominous name for a fast bowler. There was Sam Parr too, a minor cricketer but a cheerful jester who helped things along with his jokes. Once he went too far, for he put a dead mouse in the hat of the great William Caffyn, a tall silk hat that went on tour simply to appear on Sundays.

It must have been a great moment for a boy of fifteen to become, if only for a single match and as an honorary member, one of that illustrious company, to hear their jokes and know them as men of flesh and blood, and not merely as legendary and distant heroes. We can imagine him as feeling a little like Tom Brown when suddenly summoned by Young Brooke to the Sixth Form Room and told to sit down and have some supper. 'And the fifth form boy next him filled him a tumbler of bottled beer, and he ate and drank, listening to the pleasant talk, and wondering how soon he should be in the fifth, and one of that much envied society.' Lord Cobham ('C. G.' of the great Lyttelton clan), writing of W. G. when he was a year older, described him as being 'in marked contrast with his brother E. M., quiet and shy in manner.' Even when he had become an national institution, and had in him so much of heartiness and simple, jovial fun, he yet seemed capable of relapsing almost into shyness, and there was never anyone more entirely devoid of 'swagger'. Yet I do not think that we need fancy him, even at fifteen and thrust into this awe-inspiring company, as being nervous as far as cricket was concerned. He always had magnificent nerves, and an attitude towards the game full of resolution and serenity and plain common sense. By his own statement he had felt very 'anxious' when he had faced Jackson and Tarrant for the first time, but that was over and he had given his proofs. The boy was probably very like the man, who always wanted to do well and wanted to win, but never agonised.

In this match W. G. batted sixth man, which he considered 'rather a high compliment in so strong a team,' though today we find it hard to imagine him going in anywhere but first. In half an hour he made fifteen, and then he was run out by John Lillywhite,

*Stalwarts of the All-England XI, 1863. The man marked '11' is not W.G., but is standing next to him. It is the youngster in the cap, marked '12', who is William Gilbert Grace, aged 15, making his England debut against the Lansdown Club, Bath. This is the earliest photograph of Grace as a cricketer. Also in the team, but not included in this picture, is W.G.'s eldest brother, Henry.*

who was hitting the Lansdown bowling more or less as he pleased. However, as he says, 'I did not mind that: I had played for the All-England Eleven.'

Soon after came another event, not so great as far as pure cricket was concerned, but obviously exciting. This was a first match in London, and, as far as we know, a first sight of London too. I wonder if as he went there he thought of how his adventurous grandfather used to go there in his kite carriage. Probably he thought about nothing but the game and what sort of wicket there would be at the Oval. He was to play for the South Wales Club against the Surrey Club at the Oval and the Gentlemen of Sussex at Brighton. The elder Graces had played a good deal in South Wales, as they had played everywhere in the west where there was cricket. E. M. had not come back in time from Australia, so Henry suggested that W. G. should take his place and chaperoned him to

London. It was just as well, because, when they got there, the South Wales captain asked whether the boy would mind standing out of the Sussex match as there was the chance of getting 'a very good player' in his stead. Henry was not having anything of this sort, and blazed up in defence of the family: his brother should play in both matches or none, and, he added, 'I only hope every member of the team will do as well as I expect him to do.' The captain collapsed, W. G. made 5 and 38, and no more was heard of the 'very good player'. The team went on to Brighton, and Henry was not playing; the boy had to do any sticking up for himself that was necessary. He hoped that E. M. would turn up, straight from the boat, to support him, but E. M. went home to Gloucestershire. The family honour was perfectly safe: W. G. went in first wicket and made 170, and 56 not out in the second innings. South Wales asked him to play again, and he made three more good scores, against the M.C.C. and the I Zingari. By the end of the season he had made over 1,000 runs. If a boy hovering on sixteen were to do anything approaching this today, headlines would shriek of him, and his father and mother would tell the reporters, all too eagerly, how he had hit his nurse's bowling about the nursery landing. Perhaps they knew better how to treat boys in those days. A dozen cautious words in John Lillywhite's *Companion* at the end of the season announced that 'Mr. W. G. Grace promises to be a good bat: bowls very fairly.'

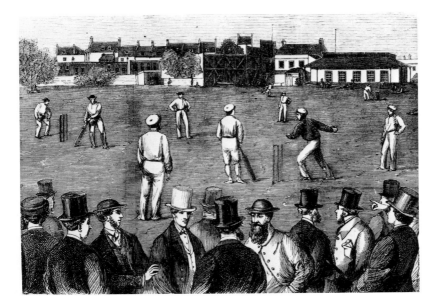

*The Oval as it appeared in the 1860s.*

# 3   1865-1872

THERE was another winter to be got through somehow, helped on its slow course perhaps by much cricket with Fred in the stable-yard; Fred, who was being just as precocious, and now at thirteen had almost forgotten his first far-distant match in which, at the age of nine, he had clean-bowled ten wickets. 1865 was to be a memorable summer in which the boy of sixteen was to play regularly in first-class cricket, and the tide, which had set so long and so fiercely against the Gentlemen, was to turn with his coming against the Players. W. G. was still quite a boy, but he was a very big boy, for he was more than six feet in height and weighed eleven stone, tall and lanky, with no premonition of the massive splendour that was to grow on him; indeed he had, according to Lord Cobham, 'some appearance of delicacy.' Already there was a black scrub upon his chin, and he seems never to have shaved till 1870 or 1871. Then he made the effort for a year or two, before finally letting his mighty beard blow where it listed. The leanness and lankiness are worth emphasising, because W. G. was in those days a very good runner and won many prizes. We think of him now as fielding at point, a very fine point, but never to be compared, by those who knew, with the cat-like E. M. When he first burst on the world, he was magnificent in the outfield, alike through his pace and his great power of throwing. Indeed one famous cricketer who played with him in those days declared, in an illuminating paradox, that the really good part of W. G.'s cricket was his fielding.

I must soon come to a point where I shall be overwhelmed in scores and averages. As the years go on and on, with their harvests of runs and wickets, I shall have, in despair, to refer the earnest student to more statistical works than this can be; but we may still mark the rungs of the ladder while there is still some climbing to be done before the boy has blossomed into the champion and been given Alfred Mynn's pads as the only one worthy to wear them.

In the summer of 1865 there were seven counties which may be said to have contended very roughly and unofficially for a championship; Notts, Surrey, Middlesex, Kent, Sussex, Yorkshire, and Cambridgeshire, while a small and inferior band, Bucks, Hants, and Warwickshire, had, as Mr. Angelo Cyrus Bantam said of the tradesmen at Bath, 'an amalgamation of themselves.' Cambridgeshire, by the way, only played three matches, and was no doubt largely dependent on its famous three – Tarrant, Hayward, and Carpenter – when they could get them away from the wandering professional teams. The All-England, the United All-England, and the United South were all more or less flourishing, but they were coming to a decadent time of their history in which the northern players declined to play on one ground and the southern players on another, and there were all sorts of schisms and wheels within wheels, such as there seem nearly always to be in professional teams which are captained by professionals. Gloucestershire as a county side did not yet exist, and so all the Graces' first-class cricket had to be played away from home, involving much travelling, and, necessarily, a good deal of expense. Exactly how the expenses were met we do not now know, but no doubt the money was more or less mysteriously forthcoming, as it always was later. When amateurs are good enough, the gate will find a way.

W. G. began this season as one who 'promised to be a good bat'; when it ended he had played twice for the Gentlemen against the Players, once for the Gentlemen of the South, and once for England against Surrey; in short he had gained all the representative honours open to him. He had caught up, if he had not actually passed, E. M., who, by the way, nearly distinguished himself this summer by causing a free fight at the Oval. Something had to be done to get Jupp out, and E. M. conceived the luminous notion of pitching a lob high in the air so that it descended on the top of the stumps. The Graces were always resourceful, but the

*Photo of the "Grace Family" taken about 1867 at KNOLE PARK ALMONDSBURY £10*

W.G.   UNKNOWN   DR HM Grace (Henry)   DR E.M.   G RUNING   ALFRED POCOCK
UNKNOWN   H HENRY   W POCOCK COUSIN   S F & RACE   DR ALFRED   R BROTHERHOOD

*A Pride of Graces. Dr. Henry Grace, in black, with grey topper, sits behind his five cricketing sons, W.G., Henry, E.M., Alfred, and G.F. The date is 1867, and W.G., far left, appears beardless. On the right of the photograph, with beard and white cap, sits Uncle Pocock.*

crowd did not this time approve of E. M.'s ingenuity; the match was stopped, and players tore up the wickets as weapons, but, in the end, Jupp had to go, and his side, the United South, was duly beaten.

W. G. began by playing for the Gentlemen of the South against the Players of the South at the Oval. He was stumped for a duck, but he bowled unchanged through both innings, and took thirteen wickets for 84 runs. This state of things seems almost contrary to the laws of nature, but it was not thought so then, and it was probably his bowling that gained him his place. Mr. C. E. Green saw him for the first time in that match, and thus describes his bowling: 'His arm was as high as his shoulder – that is as high as it was then allowed by cricket law – and while his delivery was a nice one, his action was quite different to what it was in his later days; it was more slinging and his pace was fast medium. He had not then acquired any of his subsequent craftiness with the ball. He used to bowl straight on the wicket, trusting to the ground to do the rest.' It was his bowling again that was the most distinguished in his first Gentlemen and Players match at the Oval – seven wickets for 125, as against 23 and 12 not out. At Lord's he went in first with E. M., and made 34 in the second innings; he was run out in the first innings, and if this was E. M.'s fault it was probably a good thing that he was by seven years the elder brother. These two also went in first together for England against Surrey, and made 80 for the first wicket.

Of the two Gentlemen and Players matches, the Gentlemen lost at the Oval but won at Lord's. There were fine batsmen on the Gentlemen's side, for, besides the Graces, there were I. D. Walker, R. A. H. Mitchell, and C. F. Buller, and these are great names. The fact that after long lean years the amateurs began to hold their own again was not all due to one man, but it is significant that the tide turned. The hour had come, and the man. The professionals had always depended a great deal on their bowling, and, with the bad wickets to help them, this had been much more than enough: they had perhaps a little neglected their batting, as they could afford to do. Soon they were to face a scoring machine such as they had never dreamed of, and, in addition, a fine hostile spirit that rose to its highest on the great occasion of the year. That 'promises to be a good bat' of John Lillywhite's was for the Players the writing on the wall.

In 1866 the Players won at Lord's, and the Gentlemen at the Oval, with W. G. more successful as a bowler than as a batsman. The Players had not yet felt the full scourge of his bat, but one county did; Surrey tried to play England; no county tried the experiment again for eleven years, and then the county was that of the Graces. England won the toss, and W. G. went in third wicket down. They were all out for 521, and the boy, now just eighteen, carried his bat out for 224. It was his first hundred in first-class cricket, and it was characteristic of him that he made a thorough job of it. Not for him the light heart when the first hundred was made, nor the touch of mercy towards the bowling; he was never tired of making runs, and went on piling them up with a cheerful ruthlessness. There used to be an old gentleman at St. Andrews whose golfing maxim was, 'When I am five up, I strive to be six up: when I am six up, I strive to be seven up.' W. G. would highly have

*Great innings dese*
*commemorating. Whilst still in*
*teens W.G. was gaining trophies*
*his memorable feats. The two*
*with silver shields were presente*
*him by Surrey Cricket Club for*
*innings of 173 not out in 1866,*
*for his innings of 268 of 1871.*
*curved bat on the right, as use*
*eighteenth-century cricket, is pa*
*his collect*

approved of that; with him the appetite for runs came in the making of them. His own memories of this innings were of feeling slightly nervous at the beginning of it, and then, after a blank, of the shouting at the end. The Surrey wickets fell fast before Willsher and Wootton, and England won by an innings and nearly 300 runs. On the last day, Mr. V. E. Walker allowed the young hero to go away to the Crystal Palace to run in a hurdle race. It seems a little casual, and W. G., afterwards at any rate, thought so himself. 'I know what I should say,' he remarked, 'if I were the captain.'

Three weeks or so later there came a second innings of over a hundred – 173 not out for the Gentlemen of the South against the Players of the South at the Oval; his recollection of it was that there was 'more hitting in it than in the previous match,' and that he 'played more confidently.' That 173 was out of a total of under 300, while the great innings against Surrey had represented nearly half his side's score. That is worth remarking, because W. G.'s scores in his youth constantly represented so very large a proportion of the whole side's. As Alfred Shaw, when an old man, said of him, he started so quickly, he hit the ball so hard, he travelled at such an even pace: other men might be not out 70 by lunch, W. G. was not out 130. Scoring as a whole was not large when he began to alter men's notions of what was possible; the great professional batsmen of the All-England Eleven had been content with averages of 20 or a little over. Gradually batting improved, and, still more markedly, the wickets improved, but W. G.'s long innings were colossal as compared with those of the rest of the side. This is a fact patent to anyone who looks at the scores, and it needs emphasising when any attempt is made to compare him with modern batsmen. Incidentally this innings of 173, which he called 'one of my best,' had been preceded by his taking seven of the Players' wickets, and bowling right through their innings.

Of the wickets on which W. G. was making these scores, something may here be said. Speaking of wickets in general in the early 'sixties, he himself wrote this: 'Up to this time many of the principal grounds were so rough as to be positively dangerous to play upon, and batsmen were constantly damaged by the fast bowling. When the wickets were in this condition the batsman had to look out for shooters and leave the bumping balls to look after themselves. In the 'sixties it was no unusual thing to have two or three shooters in an over; nowadays you scarcely get one shooter in a season. At this time the Marylebone ground was in a very unsatisfactory condition – so unsatisfactory that in 1864 Sussex refused to play at Lord's owing to the roughness of the ground. When I first played there the creases were not chalked out, but were actually cut out of the turf one inch deep, and about one inch wide. As matches were frequently being played, and no pains were taken to fill up the holes, it is quite easy to imagine what a terrible condition the turf presented.' He added that he could remember the time when he could go on to the pitch and pick up a handful of small pieces of gravel. In 1865 a large piece of the ground was levelled and returfed. Lord's gradually improved, but in 1870 it was still capable of an almost murderous condition. It was in that year that he made an historic 66 against Freeman and Emmett. 'Tom Emmett and I,' said Freeman, many years afterwards, 'have often said it was a marvel that the Doctor was not either maimed or unnerved for the rest of his days or killed outright. I often think of his pluck when I watch a modern batsman scared if a medium-paced ball hits him on the hand; he should have seen our expresses flying about his ribs, shoulders and head in 1870.'

With the end of 1866, W. G., now eighteen years old, was fairly established as what Pierce Egan would have called a 'non-pareil and an out-and-outer.' He was no longer climbing the ladder; he had got to the top, although he was still destined to add a few more rungs to it, dizzy rungs utterly beyond anyone else's reach. Henceforth he had great, greater, and greatest years, but they no longer belong to the making of a champion, and so can be taken in the less detail. It is rather odd, by the way, that though he had made such a name in the south it was not till 1866 that W. G. had played in the north. In that year he captained eighteen Colts of Nottingham and Sheffield against the All-England Eleven. The north were to know more about him in a very short while. 1867, which was interrupted by scarlet fever in the very middle of the summer, was not a great batting year, and had not a single century in it, but it was, he considered, his 'most successful bowling year'. After reading that, it is curious to turn to the averages and see that he took only 131 wickets at 13.12 apiece, but the numbers both of overs and wickets were much smaller than we are used to today. Wootton bowled a larger number of overs and took 152 wickets, but no one else approached his total bag, and the two illustrious persons that came second and third on the list, J. C. Shaw and Alfred Shaw, had but 36 and 43 wickets to their names respectively.

1868 was generally a great run-getting year, in which the complaint was heard, possibly for the first time, that the bat held an

*The great Alfred Shaw*

*W. G. Grace at 20*

unfair advantage over the ball. W. G. went in first wicket for the Gentlemen at Lord's, and made 134 not out. The whole side made 201, and B. B. Cooper's 28 was the only other double-figure score. W. G. described it 'one of the very best innings I ever played as the ground was very bad and difficult and the bowling very good.' The fact that Pooley had a longstop is eloquent, and 'many good length balls flew over the wicket keeper's head.' Later, at Canterbury, W. G. joined William Lambert on his then solitary pinnacle, by making a hundred in each innings. This was for South against North of the Thames, and despite his efforts the South were beaten. Fred made his first appearance at Lord's for England against the M.C.C.: he was seventeen, and equalled his brother's record.

At about this time there seems to have been some question of W. G. going up to Cambridge, and Caius, having a great medical tradition, was to have been his college. Oxford, too, had tried to tempt him, but their blandishments were even less successful. Mr. C. E. Green, who went down in 1868, said, in the *Memorial Biography*, that rumour of W. G.'s coming caused great excitement among the Cambridge cricketers of that time, as well it might. How far the negotiations went, it is now impossible to discover, but years afterwards, in answer to a question of Mr. Green's, W. G. said, 'Yes, I really came very near doing so.' It is believed that his father put a stop to the plan by saying that he must stick to his medical studies at home. If he had gone to Cambridge,

*A memorable enrolment on October 7th, 1868, at the Bristol Medical School*

| No. | Date. | Name. | Term. | Remarks. |
|---|---|---|---|---|
| | | *Winter* **Session, 18**68 – 69 | | |
| | | **Class of** *General Perpetual Students.* | | |
| 1 | Oct. 1 | Albert Barnes Rees | | P.º £23 12 6 |
| 2 | " 3 | John Sprod | | P.º £23 12 6 |
| 3 | " " | William John Cole | | P.º £23 12 6 |
| 4 | " " | William Allen Sturge | | P.º |
| 5 | " 7 | William Gilbert Grace | | P.º £23 12 6 |
| 6 | " 15 | Benjamin Jones Messiah | | P.º £23 12 6 |

we should probably have lost one piece of cricket history: the name of Cobden might have been long forgotten, Mr. Robert Lyttelton might not have written his immortal passage about Mr. Charles Marsham's umbrella, and there would not have arisen the question, never to be solved in this world, whether it was Bourn or Scott who fielded the first ball of the most famous over ever bowled. If W. G. had been on the Cambridge side in 1870, it is highly improbable that any hat-trick of Cobden's would have been needed to pull the match out of the fire. That is so glorious a memory that Caius's loss may be said to be the cricketing world's gain. Moreover, W. G.'s interposition would have seemed almost as unfair as did that of the gods on one side or the other in Homer. Cambridge has never wanted any divine loading of the dice in order to beat Oxford.

In 1869, W. G. became thoroughly outrageous, making nine centuries, six of them in first-class matches. He was elected a member of the M.C.C. early in the year, and at once went to Oxford, on a first visit, and made a hundred for the club. This was two years before he signalised his first match at Cambridge in a similar manner. The succinct comment on that second occasion may be quoted here out of its turn: 'W. N. Powys was expected to slaughter us. He did not.' He was to repeat these feats of ruthlessness against undergraduates many times afterwards. Doubtless Oxford tried as hard as ever did Mr. Ward at Cambridge, with his breakfasts and his Bollinger, to mitigate this severity, and doubtless the challenge was as vain as it was gaily accepted. If the sometimes sceptical northerners had wanted any further proof of W. G.'s capacity, they had it this year, when he went to Sheffield to play for the South against the North, and in the first innings made 122 out of 173 against Freeman, Wootton, and Emmett. It was after this that Emmett, who had not hitherto whole-heartedly prostrated himself before the new idol, remarked, 'I call him a non-such; he ought to be made to play with a littler bat.'

There were more big scores in 1870, two for the newly arisen Gloucestershire. The county had first played a match, against Devonshire, as far back as 1862, and Dr. Grace had subsequently got up several more or less casual county matches, but, though he was always anxious to form a regular county club, he had not succeeded in doing so till 1870, the year before he died. It appears that the earliest minutes of the club are lost, but it was undoubtedly flourishing and on a firm basis in 1873, since there has lately been

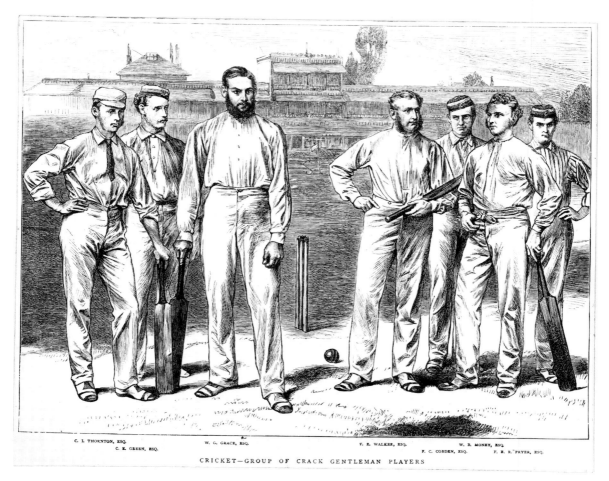

C. I. THORNTON, ESQ.

C. E. GREEN, ESQ.

W. G. GRACE, ESQ.

V. E. WALKER, ESQ.

W. R. MONEY, ESQ.

F. C. COBDEN, ESQ.

F. E. R. FRYER, ESQ.

CRICKET—GROUP OF CRACK GENTLEMAN PLAYERS

*By 1871, when this engraving was made, W. G. Grace was already outstanding amongst the other Gentlemen, illustrated here at Lords.*

published, in the *Bristol Evening World*, a letter written in that year by E. M. as secretary. The county had then arranged six matches, and had an impressive list of officers, beginning with the Duke of Beaufort as President and Lord Fitzhardinge as Vice-President.

To go back to 1870, W. G. played two long innings in that year for the Gentlemen against the poor Players, for whom at this time one begins to be positively sorry. They got him out cheaply in the first innings at the Oval, but he made 215 in the second. The Players saved that match, but lost by four runs at Lord's, where W. G. made 109 out of 187 in the first innings. It had been a good year, 'one of my best,' but 1871 was to be 'my most successful.' It was not quite so dramatic perhaps as 1876, with its thousand runs in August and the Yorkshire bowlers going on strike, nor as that wonderful Indian summer, yet far away, with its thousand runs in May at the age of forty-seven (how incredible an age forty-seven must have seemed then); but for a rich, continuous stream of runs, flowing from spring to autumn, it was never to be beaten again.

There were ten centuries in it, and that in a year when the weather was not very fine nor the wickets very good. Some of them were much more than hundreds, for, says the maker of them, 'I never lost patience': that insatiable appetite never grew jaded. Three of these big scores were in benefit matches; W. G.'s value to a beneficiary was, of course, incalculable, and to make runs for his friends was a good turn of a sort which particularly appealed to him. Willsher was the first, with Single *v.* Married at Lord's, and he had bad luck in his weather, but, still, W. G. had time to make 189 for him, and also got up another match later in the year, in which he made most of the runs, bowled throughout both innings, and was never out of the field for a single moment. Next came Stephenson's match, North *v.* South at the Oval, and with the first ball of the match W. G. was given out l.b.w. to an enemy from whom he was never quite safe, J. C. Shaw. It must have been a very clear case, and John Lillywhite a very conscientious umpire. 'For once,' was W. G.'s comment, 'I am bound to say I think the verdict was right.' The second and third day brought their revenge, for he made 260 out of 436, 'paying particular attention to J. C. Shaw.' Perhaps that was the occasion on which Shaw said, 'I puts 'em where I like and he puts 'em where he likes.' At any rate it will serve as well as another.

The third was at Brighton, for the Gentlemen against the Players (who had hitherto escaped their annual flogging), for the benefit of John Lillywhite. Once more the tactless J. C. Shaw had him out in the first over, this time clean bowled. Lillywhite may have thought it a judgment on him for that remorseless decision at the Oval. We can imagine J. C. Shaw's demeanour from Daft's pleasant account of him. There he stood, in his shirt of broad black-and-white stripes, looking for a moment at the great man's stumps sprawling; then he put his hands in his pockets, and his face took on 'a vacant expression as though he were contemplating something that was taking place on the distant horizon.' The story of Lillywhite's bargain is well known. He handed W. G. two sovereigns, and told him to repay sixpence for every run he made in the second innings. For an over or two, W. G. played himself in carefully; for the first hundred runs or so he remembered the mounting sixpences, and then he forgot everything in another delicious revenge on J. C. Shaw. At the end of the day he had made 200 not out, and was met by Lillywhite with a demand for £5 on account. The money was paid on condition that there should be no further claims or there would be a hit wicket the first thing next

*. G. Grace with Henry Jupp, the
sman who came nearest to Grace
throughout the 1870s*

morning. In point of fact, when the next morning came, he made
only another eight and sixpence worth of runs, so Lillywhite had
few regrets. At the end of that summer, W. G. had made 2,390
runs for an average of 78.9. There were other great batsmen
playing, Daft and Carpenter and Jupp, E. M. and Fred Grace and
Yardley, A. N. Hornby and I. D. Walker, but the best average
among them all was Daft's 37.10. Figures can sometimes be very
eloquent things. Well might I. D. Walker say, 'W. G. has not the
style of Mitchell, Alfred Labbock, or Buller, but as a bat he is

worth all the three put together.' Moreover, as a minor enterprise, W. G. had bowled 738 overs and taken 78 wickets at just over 16 runs apiece, and only one bowler, Southerton, had taken over a hundred.

1872, the next year, provided, as it was almost bound to do, a small set-back, an average of only 57; but once again W. G. dealt faithfully with the Players, and scored two hundreds and a seventy against them in the course of a week, to say nothing of another hundred for England against Notts and Yorkshire. In this summer he and his brother Fred played several matches for the United South Eleven, which, except for the Graces, consisted almost entirely of professionals. He was, of course, an immense attraction for any such touring eleven, and there was no pretence that he was not paid for playing in it. He collected the team, paid the players, and received a stated amount for each match under a legal agreement, with a penalty clause.

# 4 1872 & 1873

1873 was another of the outstanding years – a batting average of 71, and 55 wickets at 17 apiece. There is always a temptation to forget the bowling, and yet, even apart from its great intrinsic value to his side, it has to be remembered as emphasising W. G.'s astonishing vitality. As he always went in first, he had constantly to bat, with no interval for rest, after a long spell of bowling. Whether or not he could have made more runs is an unanswerable question; one is sometimes tempted to think it impossible, but at any rate the testimony to his stamina is amazing. Already he was no light weight, and when he was still in his twenties he weighed fifteen stone. That is something even for inexhaustible youth to carry about under a hot sun. The Players were chosen once more for special castigation, and so were the Players of the North and the Players of the South. They were all impartially dealt with in the matter of centuries. In three matches against the Players, at Lord's, the Oval, and Prince's, W. G. averaged 130. Mr. Yardley, in a footnote in *The History of a Hundred Centuries*, says, 'No wonder the poor Players dubbed him the Demon.' That name has since been given to another, F. R. Spofforth, and was much more physically appropriate in his case. A famous old St. Andrews golfer of the early 'seventies, Mr. Mitchell Innes, once said that the way to beat a professional was never to let him get a hole up. W. G. had

*The Atlantic crossing in 1872*

never heard of golf in those days; but, if he had, he would have approved this advice, for he certainly lived up to it; he never took his iron heel off the Players' necks. They, poor down-trodden ones, had added to them that summer, though they did not yet appreciate their good fortune, one who was going to do much to redress the batting inequality. In April a seventeen-year-old colt called Arthur Shrewsbury, who probably walked to the Trent Bridge Ground with a thick scarf round his neck and an odd little billycock hat perched on his head, looking wonderfully unlike a cricketer, patiently defied Alfred Shaw, J. C. Shaw, McIntyre, and Morley till he had made 35 runs against that magnificent array of bowlers. The time was to come when W. G., asked who, leaving himself out of the argument, was the greatest batsman of his time, was to answer, unhesitatingly, 'Give me Arthur.' The counties of these two supreme batsmen, Gloucestershire and Notts, were equal this year at the head of the counties, and the Gloucester side was an entirely amateur one.

At the end of the season of 1873, W. G. went to Australia, and a short account of his doings there may be combined with those in Canada of the year before. Most people are apt nowadays to think of him as a stay-at-home cricketer, a permanent bulwark against which for years and years the tired waves of the invaders spent themselves. Since his day so many teams have gone to Australia, and we have lived through such long agonies of waiting for their fate in the evening paper that we grow forgetful. Yet, in fact, W. G. invaded Australia twice, and Canada and the United States once.

*W.G. is shown characteristically in the centre of the stage in this painting of his Canadian tour. He is shown with his colleagues in Montreal, 1872.*

Probably the Canadian trip of 1872 – it was a light-hearted enterprise – is best remembered now on account of one story. W. G., having to make a speech at the first banquet at which the side was entertained, replied in these remarkable words, 'Gentlemen, I beg to thank you for the honour you have done me. I never saw better bowling than I have seen to-day, and I hope to see as good wherever I go.' He was then struck by the brilliant notion that this form of words was capable of endless adaptation, and so he went on, much to his own and everyone else's satisfaction, with 'better batting,' 'better wicket,' 'prettier ladies,' and, in America, 'better oysters'. Each variation has been faithfully recorded by Mr. Fitzgerald, who captained the side. W. G. liked simple jokes, and this one appealed to him alike for its simplicity and its practical utility, so that years afterwards, when the menace of oratory became imminent, he would say, 'I think I must give them one of my Canadian speeches.'

The tour, of which a full account may be read in *W. G.*, hardly needs detailed record now. It consisted of cricket matches against rather inexpert twenty-twos, with much friendliness on the part of the Canadian hosts, many banquets, some casual shooting and fishing expeditions, and the offer of two young bears for the champion to take home with him, which he discreetly declined. The names of the English team are worth setting out, because it was a very good one indeed, perhaps rather too good for its task, representative or very nearly so of the Gentlemen of their time; R. A. Fitzgerald, W. G. Grace, Alfred and Edgar Lubbock, A. N.

*The 'passport' photograph of 1872*

Hornby, the Hon. George Harris (afterwards Lord Harris), C. J. Ottaway, W. H. Hadow, C. K. Francis, F. Pickering, A. Appleby, and W. M. Rose. W. G., of course, made most of the runs, while Appleby, with his fast left-hand bowling, and Rose, an admirable foil and complement to him with his lobs, dealt out death and destruction to the Canadian batsmen. Rose was so successful that W. G. grew a little jealous in a friendly way, and, insisting that he could diddle them out just as cheaply, took later on to bowling at the other end to Appleby. The team crossed over to America, where cricket was not as moribund, or perhaps one should say as dead, as it is now, and played at New York, Philadelphia, and Boston. Parr and Willsher had earlier taken teams there, and there was an excited if not an instructed public for the game. Baseball players were taken into the cricketers' ranks, and their fielding immensely impressed W. G. Indeed the fielding was so good that it was very hard work to get the ball through a network of twenty-two men. Moreover, there was at Philadelphia a very fine fast bowler, Newhall, whom W. G. called 'one of the best I ever played against.' So, besides severe banqueting, there was some much harder work than in Canada. The match at Philadelphia had a bloodcurdling finish. The Englishmen went in to get 33 runs to win, and they got them, but they lost seven wickets in doing it, and, try as they would, could not get the ball through the fielding ring. W. G. took an hour to make seven runs, and when he was caught off Newhall the air was blackened with the hats and umbrellas of

*Two members of the Canadian touring party were taken sightseeing to Niagara Falls. They are C. K. Francis, seated left, and W.G., on the ground, amongst the ladies.*

delirious spectators. Almost anything might have happened till Appleby came in and settled matters with a gallant boundary. Much the same thing seemed likely to occur at Boston, where the wicket was a quagmire, the fieldsmen up to their ankles in slush, and the game went on so late that no one could see. The Boston umpires sturdily refused all appeals against the light till a ball, of the proximity of which he was wholly unaware, hit Fitzgerald on the toe. Then it was agreed that the game had gone on long enough.

A year later, in 1873, W. G. undertook to take a team out to Australia, and, though several whom he asked could not come, notably Hornby, Yardley, and Alfred Shaw, it was a good team, with a strong family and Gloucestershire flavour, W. G. and G. F. Grace, W. R. Gilbert, J. A. Bush, F. H. Boult, Greenwood, Jupp, Humphrey, J. Lillywhite, Oscroft, McIntyre, and Southerton.

This was a very different enterprise from that in Canada, and not, as one gathers, by any means such an enjoyable one. The welcome indeed was overwhelming: there were banquets in plenty; governors and mayors and speeches – too many speeches. Often when the team visited, as it did several times, a remote place, it was met twenty miles short of the town by a welcoming troop of horsemen. They made their way along, like some prize-fighting hero of old, 'surrounded by a cavalcade of noblemen and gentlemen.' Brass bands played them through the streets. The hospitality was of the kindest, but some of the hosts seemed to think that hospitality stopped short as soon as the cricket field was reached: then friends became deadly foes and must look out for themselves. It is a point of view by no means yet extinct in Australia, and, however much we may admire the keenness from which it springs, it does not make for a pleasant game. The account of the tour in Lillywhite for 1875, attributed to Fred Grace, is perfectly plain-spoken on the point: 'The trip, on the whole, was an enjoyable one, as far as seeing Colonies and meeting good friends; but in a cricketing point of view it was NOT a good one. We were met in a bad spirit, as if contending cricketers were enemies.'

Now the Grace family, as has been said, was not one to knuckle under or to forgo what it believed to be its rights. Of W. G. it might be said, as Brian de Bois-Guilbert's squire said of his master, 'He knows how to requite scorn with scorn and blows with blows, as well as courtesy with courtesy.' So there were protracted arguments about the rolling or not rolling of the wicket, and once the English team was taken off the field by its captain because, when the new batsman came in, the old one obstinately refused to go out.

'He was the Australian of Australians,' Mr. Cardus has written of Spofforth; 'a stark man that let in with him the coldest blast of antagonism that ever blew over a June field.' Something of that hostile atmosphere hung round his first meeting with W. G. The champion was batting against all comers, in the nets, at the Melbourne. An unknown young bowler 'lolled up two or three balls in a funny slow way,' and then suddenly let loose one of his fastest. Down went the stumps, and the batsman called out, 'Where did that one come from?' but the bowler had slipped away to bide his time.

Rather typical, too, is the picture of Boyle coming to Melbourne with his 1,500 supporters from Bendigo. He would not bowl to the great man at the net, but stood and watched, and presently remarked, 'If I could get a ball in between his leg and the wicket, I could get him.' When the match began next day, Boyle was put on after W. G. had made some runs: he did get that ball between his leg and the wicket, and he did get him, and all the 1,500 men of Bendigo cooeed in triumphant chorus, while Allan the other bowler fell on Boyle and hugged him. That first match against eighteen of Melbourne was disastrous, for the team had not got rid of its sea legs, and was beaten in an innings. Moreover, Boyle and Allan, who was called 'the bowler of the century,' were, in fact, very fine bowlers. A local paper, which appears to have left behind it some legitimate descendants, said that the team were 'arrant

*W.G. photographed in 1873 with his younger brother Fred, seated, and the great professional bowler Southerton*

duffers', but, in the next match at Ballarat, W. G. revenged himself on Allan with a hard-hit hundred, and, generally speaking, the team had the better of the fifteens and eighteens it met. The Australian bowling was good, and gave promise of what it would accomplish five years later in England, but the batting was still weak, and the wickets were not yet good.

*51*

Apart from the big matches at Melbourne and Sydney, there were some rather farcical ones on farcical wickets, of which a full account may be studied in *W. G.* At one place a ball was bowled but the wicket was such that it never reached the batsman at all. At another, stones were picked up in basketfuls on the wicket, and some of the pitches had been ploughed fields but a short time before. Sea voyages that made everybody ill, and hundred-mile coach drives over rudimentary roads, led up to these matches, and even the escorting cavalcades can hardly have compensated. Sometimes the matches were finished too soon, because nobody could make many runs, but the promoters had engaged their brass bands and advertised three days' cricket, and insisted on their pound of flesh, eked out by single-wicket matches. It sounds, it cannot be denied, an exhausting and depressing experience, but W. G. was quite inexhaustible and not easily depressed. He wrote of it, long afterwards to be sure, with an amused tolerance, and he had some shooting and fishing and a kangaroo hunt. He had taken his wife with him; indeed the tour was really an extension of his honeymoon, for he had been married not long before setting out. Mrs. Grace, however, did not share in the more prostrating adventures, and stayed with friends in the big towns. The scores were telegraphed home – an exciting innovation, and a rather tiresome gentleman, who made a speech at lunch during one of the matches, spent a considerable time in explaining that he had long since prophesied this marvel.

# 5

# 1874-1879

The year 1874 was a very good if not a positively terrific one, and included the usual hundred against the Players, this time at Prince's. They must have been getting well accustomed to it, but they probably never liked it, and this time, believing themselves to have a grievance, they ended an unpleasant match in a unpleasant state of mind. W. G. himself describes the occasion, perhaps with some economy of historic accuracy, as 'one of the remarkably few instances of a difference of opinion between my opponents and myself.' W. G. and G. F. were batting together in the Gentlemen's second innings. The score was about 130 for two; W. G. was well set, and this circumstance was the more irritating because he had been missed at long-leg by Humphrey. Fred Grace played a ball back to the bowler, James Lillywhite, and would have been easily caught and bowled but that W. G. was in the way, and to run round him involved too great a detour. There were frantic appeals to both umpires for obstruction, but they were answered in the batsman's favour. Fred Grace only made a dozen, but W. G. made 110. This rankled, and when, later, Daft was given out l.b.w. to W. G.'s bowling, he received the verdict with pronounced disfavour. The Grace family between them got all the wickets; the Players were all out for 128, and lost the match and their tempers.

1875 was wet and cold, and nobody made many runs; no less than six people had the temerity to be above W. G. in the averages, and he was popularly believed, goodness knows how absurdly, to have 'gone off.' Nobody alleged that his bowling had gone off, for he took 192 wickets at just over 12 runs apiece. Alfred Shaw bowled fifty more overs and took thirty less wickets. Whether W. G. had deteriorated or not was quickly decided in the next year, perhaps the most dramatic of all. The knowing ones may have said, 'I told you so,' in May, when he only made 163 runs in eight innings. In June they may have begun to doubt; in July, when he averaged 57, they must have felt small, and in August they were covered with confusion, for he played ten innings for 1,278 runs.

The eight days of blazing sunshine that were to break all records, and so many bowlers' hearts, began on the 11th of August at Canterbury, when the M.C.C. went in against Kent's big score made on the first day. The bowlers were happy, unconscious of their doom, for they got the great man out for 17, and the side out for 144. The M.C.C. followed on about five o'clock. Then the fun began. W. G. seems to have believed the match lost, and he would have been glad to get home next day to have a Sunday's rest. So he thought he would hit. 'We'll make it warm for them this time,' he observed to the late Mr. Charlie Clark, as he fastened his glove. And he did hit; but, as before, he never lost patience; no Sunday's rest was worth the taking of liberties, and by 6.45 he had made 133 not out, the whole score being 217 for four wickets. It was sunnier than ever next day, and W. G. broke his bat and had to borrow one too small in the handle, but still it was all very capital, and his bat handle was padded for him at lunch-time, and there was champagne to be had in the officers' tent, and the Kent bowlers toiled and sweated, and the fielders hoped for a chance that never came, and Mr. Absolom thought it a very hot day, and at last, something over six hours from the time he had first gone in, W. G. was caught off Lord Harris, who was perhaps growing rather cross by this time, for a little matter of 344.

There was a hot, slow cross-country journey to Bristol on the Sunday. On Monday morning Notts lost the toss at Clifton, and W. G. hit Shaw and Morley and Barnes about for just over three hours and made 177. That was on the 14th; the 15th and 16th were days of rest in the sense of bowling and fielding, and Notts were beaten by ten wickets. As they were going home, they met the Yorkshiremen coming to Cheltenham, and warned them, but Tom Emmett laughed and said that the big 'un could not do it three

*When W.G. led the Gloucester-shire team to play in Bristol, they used the Clifton College ground, shown here*

times running. Once before he had made a rash remark about waiting till he and George Freeman got W. G. to Sheffield. Now he was to learn again not to tempt the Fates too far. Yorkshire, like Notts, lost the toss, and they had over eight hours of W. G. and never got him out at all. At the end of the first day he was not out 216. Next morning it rained, but by one o'clock he was at it again, and carried his bat through the innings for 318 – 839 runs in three innings (once not out). It may have been ill-disciplined, but it was eminently natural in the Yorkshire bowlers that they refused to go on when their easy-going captain, Ephraim Lockwood, told them to. 'Why don't you make 'em?' exclaimed Emmett. 'Ain't you captain?' and seizing the ball sent down three wides running.

In the same year W. G. dallied with twenty-two of Grimsby for the United South, on a ground where the grass was rather long, to the tune of 400 not out. He also made his hardy annual – 169 – against the Players at Lord's, put Gloucestershire at the top of the county tree, and took 124 wickets. He scored 2,622 runs in first-class cricket, and the one really surprising thing about it is that his average was only 62.

In 1877, W. G. had a comparatively modest batting year, though still top of the averages, and a great bowling one, since he took 179 wickets – over thirty more than anyone else – for a fraction

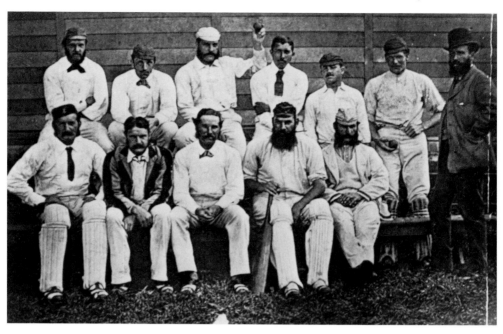

over 12 runs apiece. This year is a little unfairly dwarfed in retrospect by coming just after that stupendous 1876 and just before the first Australian invasion.

1878 is not only an historic year in cricket, it was a decisive year in the personal history of W. G. He was thirty years old, and a married man; after a somewhat leisurely and broken course of study he was nearing the position of a fully fledged doctor, and he is said to have had serious thoughts of abandoning first-class cricket in favour of his profession. How near he came to doing so it is now impossible to tell. That years afterwards he said his decision had trembled in the balance appears tolerably certain: the event which had tipped the beam in favour of cricket and against such deplorable virtue was the coming of the Australians. That he wanted to get at them no one can doubt, and perhaps his contemplated retirement was never so horribly possible as he came afterwards to believe. It is permissible to think that if the Australians had not mercifully intervened, somebody or something else would have done so. For my part I accept Mr. Webbe's verdict, expressed with a faith and fervour that no mere words can convey, 'W. G. never *could* have given up cricket.'

At any rate the Australians arrived, rugged, hirsute, and serious, and neither England in general nor W. G. in particular was very

*This contemporary engraving of the Australians playing against Thornton's XI at Orleans House in 1878 scarcely does justice to the hostility of Spofforth's bowling. The illustrator is at pains to show the Englishmen's sang froid, if not downright indifference, especially th batsman at the bowler's end and the curiously stationed umpire, whilst Spofforth, together with his fellow Australians, is shown wearing a funny hat, and long stop is made to look like a cowboy.*

much frightened of them. They had two or three fine natural batsmen, an incorruptible stone-waller, some resolute hitters with a cross bat, and four as magnificent bowlers as ever bowled together on one side. Allan, then deemed the greatest of the four, never did himself justice playing in England. There were Boyle and Garrett, and in these shaven and effeminate days it seems difficult to believe that two men so bearded could ever have bowled so well. Lastly there was Spofforth with his cold confident hostility. He was destined to be W. G.'s greatest adversary, who could admire without fear and never yielded to that feeling of inevitability which crept over J. C. Shaw. He could say, with a splendid arrogance, of all the other bowlers, 'They were a bit afraid of what he would to their balls . . . never in my case.'

It was a chilly and wet summer to make the visitors shiver, as unlike as possible to the summers they knew. Yet it may not have done them an ill turn, for their bowlers wrought havoc, and the bad wickets, by reducing all to comparative impotence, may have neutralised their batting weaknesses. To begin with they were helpless against Shaw and Morley at Trent Bridge, and people were less frightened of them than ever. Then came the memorable day at Lord's, the single day of cold and puddles and calamity, in the space of which the M.C.C. went down twice before Spofforth and Boyle (W. G. 4 and 0), and the Australians, after a first innings of 41, had to make only 12 runs to win. Of all the shocks that a complacent England has had to suffer, in all manner of fields, in the

*Alfred Bryan's caricature of W.G.,
the hero of Lords.*

*The Souvenir of the national
testimonial to W. G. Grace of 1879.
It includes a photograph and
Grace's career record to date.*

last hundred years, this, the first of them, must have been the most sudden and appalling.

Incidentally, W. G. had an amusing little quarrel with the Australians over Midwinter, who was an Australian cricketer but a Gloucestershire man by birth. He had returned to England the year before, and had promised, so W. G. asserted, to play for his county in 1878. The Australians were equally positive he had promised to play for them. One fine day in June, Gloucester was playing Surrey at the Oval; the Australians were playing Middlesex at Lord's. There were only ten men on the Gloucester side – where was Midwinter? W. G. had his suspicions; he handed over the captaincy to E. M., took a cab, and drove to Lord's. There was the faithless Midwinter, proposing to bat for the Australians. W. G.'s arguments must have been eloquent and formidable, for in less than no time Midwinter was driving back to the Oval, in custody and another cab. This was not the end of the argument, for the Australians did not approve of kidnapping; they declared they would not play against Gloucestershire without an apology, and they ultimately got it – but Gloucester had not been one short.

W. G. had a measure of revenge for the Gentlemen, and there were others who beat these gallant foes – Yorkshire, and, above all, Cambridge, with its eleven of the peerless 1878 vintage, which first filled the Australians with a lasting terror of a light-blue coat. Still the glory of the summer rested with the invaders. Even as, nearly seventy years before, Molineaux had first threatened the might of England in the ring, so now she was threatened at cricket, and it was for W. G., as another Tom Cribb, to defend her. Here was a good reason for cricketing all the summer; England had doctors enough.

In fact it was in the following year that he attained to the dignity which became so familiar in after years. It was in 1879 that the mature Dr. W. G. Grace went in first in place of the youthful hero W. G. Grace, Esquire. Yet there was – Heaven be thanked – no retiring, and any thought of it must have been put still further away by the presentation of a national testimonial – a cheque for nearly £1,500, a clock, and two bronze ornaments. There had been some question of buying W. G. a practice, but it was abandoned because, in Lord Fitzhardinge's words, 'Mr. Grace was old enough and strong enough to choose a practice for himself.' He did in fact start in practice in Bristol, and of that something will be said later, in the chapter on his private life.

# 1880-1891

THE 'eighties seem to mark the beginning of an epoch, both in the history of cricket and of its greatest figure. The Australian tourists became a regular feature of the game, and 1880 saw the first of the long series now known as Test Matches. The old wandering elevens were gone for ever, killed by the better organisation of county cricket and the wider interest taken in it. The North had finally and definitely caught up the South: Yorkshire and Lancashire were no longer new: Nottinghamshire was to dominate England and send out, from its superfluity, unwanted bowlers to strengthen poorer counties. With the continual spreading of the game there had come an equalisation of forces, and in that equalisation even W. G. was to share. He was still immensely great; still, like David Harris of Hambledon, to be 'chosen first of any man in England,' and that for years to come; his zest for the game, his tendency to change the bowling by going on himself at the other end, did not abate, but he was never again to overpower and terrify in quite the same way; there were other run-getters who could be named in the same breath with him: Arthur Shrewsbury and William Gunn had their own way, less dramatic but nearly as relentless, of breaking bowlers' hearts. As a colossal personage, he came more and more to bestride the world of cricket, but never again in quite the same degree as a player pure and simple. It was

*William Gunn* LEFT *and* ABOVE *Arthur Shrewsbury, the leading batsmen who provided the professional challenge in the 1880s.*

noteworthy that he was still top of the averages in 1880, but this was the last time in the 'eighties. Only three times had he failed to hold that place between 1866 and 1879.

It was in particular the professional batsmen, headed by Shrewsbury, who had improved, so that it was now their names that clustered round the top of the list of averages. W. G. himself, summing up the situation at the end of the 'eighties, wrote, 'We must face the fact that the professional standard of all-round play is higher today than at any time since the game began. The professionals are now the equals of the amateurs in batting and fielding, and their superiors in bowling.' Their bowling superiority was, of course, no new thing, but their type of bowling was a different one from that of W. G.'s early days. He himself had helped to kill the successors of Jackson and Tarrant; he had broken the hearts of the fast bowlers, and the 'eighties saw but few new ones arising, though one, Crossland, enjoyed a brief and brilliant career, which depended largely on the too supine nature of the umpiring. Alfred Shaw was now the great model, and it was an era of slow and medium-paced bowling of extreme accuracy.

W. G. still loomed vast and menacing, but Gloucestershire as the county of the 'all resistless Graces' had passed its zenith, for E. M. was no longer quite so young or so good as he had been, and

*G. F. Grace. He was a cricketer of astounding promise, but only played for England once, in 1880, before his tragically early death. This was the last photograph that was taken of him.*

Fred died with tragic suddenness in 1880. This was but a few weeks after the first Test Match, and it is pleasant to remember that the three brothers played together for England in the only such match in which it was possible. The Australian eleven of that year came over in rather a mysterious manner, unheralded and unorganised, with their programme to fill up as best they could on their arrival. The match against England at the Oval was only an afterthought, due largely to Mr. C. W. Alcock and Lord Harris. W. G. opened the international ball for England with 152, a score surpassed by a single run by W. L. Murdoch in Australia's second and most valiant innings, which followed a collapse in their first. In the end England won by five wickets, though they had to make only 57 to win. As Spofforth could not bowl for them, the Australians did nobly. Fred Grace made a pair of spectacles, but caught the most famous catch in all cricket, when he sent back Bonnor. So high climbed the ball that the batsmen had finished their second run ere they learnt that their labour had been vain.

Of his four brothers, Fred was the nearest to W. G. in age, and the one to whom he was most devoted. The elder brother had taken each successive step in cricket a year or two in advance, and then looked back with pride and pleasure on the younger who followed him. Fred's death made a real and permanent gap in W. G.'s life, and four years later came another. In July 1884 the two brothers were playing against Lancashire at Manchester when they received a telegram telling them of the sudden death of their mother. The match was stopped, and they hurried home. Mrs. Grace had lived to see her prophecies come more than true and her son dominate the world of cricket. She had continued to watch county matches at Clifton, and her interest in the game had remained keen to the end. Every night her sons wrote or telegraphed to her the result of the day's play, a custom which was afterwards kept up in W. G.'s own household. There cannot now be very many cricketers who saw her, but one of them at any rate, Mr. A. J. Webbe, has an engaging little memory of her. One day, I think at Canterbury, he asked W. G. if he had noticed an old lady in a red cloak watching the play. 'Why, you rascal,' was the answer, 'I believe you mean my mother.'

It would be tedious to give any lengthy record of W. G.'s doings in this middle period which came between the first heroic flush of youth and the glorious Indian summer of the 'nineties. There were comparatively lean years both in point of runs and in number of innings, for doctoring did sometimes seriously intervene. In 1882

*Mrs. Martha Grace, lifelong enthusiast for the game her family dominated*

his profession kept him out of the Gentlemen and Players match at the Oval for the first time since 1867, and the match ended in a tie. He played at Lord's, and the Gentlemen won by seven wickets.

All things are comparative, and years that we may call lean for W. G. would be rich ones for almost anyone else. A glance through the pages of *The History of a Hundred Centuries* is perhaps the quickest way of realising what a force he still was. 1881 saw him scourge the Players yet again for exactly 100 at Lord's. In 1884 he made over 100 against the Australians with Spofforth, Boyle, and Palmer, for the M.C.C., for the Gentlemen, and for Gloucestershire. In 1885 the inevitably doomed Players (when scarce another man on the Gentlemen's side could make a run), Yorkshire, Surrey, and Middlesex were the sufferers, and against Middlesex

*W. G. Grace l.b.w. bowled Palmer 101, for the MCC against the Australians at Lords, May 1884.*

his innings was thoroughly typical of old times – 221 out of 348, and not out at the end of it. In 1886 the Australians came back, and there were two more hundreds against them, including 170 in the Oval Test Match – 'not altogether faultless but still I think I may fairly say without undue egotism a pretty good performance.' In 1887 he nearly made two hundreds against Yorkshire – first

*The Gloucestershire team in the 1880s. On W.G.'s right hand is E. M. Grace, his initials woven in his sweater. Seated in front of W. is his cousin, W. R. Gilbert.*

*Gentlemen v Players at Lords, 1891. The Players take the field. Grace, who led the Gentlemen, watches from the members' stand.*

innings 92, and 193 not out in the second; against Kent he did make a hundred in each innings. In 1888, his fortieth year, he did the same thing against Yorkshire – 143 and 153 (but there was no Emmett there this time to suffer), and he made 165 against Turner and Ferris for the Gentlemen. Finally, in 1889, he made two hundreds for Gloucestershire and one for the South against the North at Scarborough, when we may be tolerably sure he had not fallen into the vulgar error of going to bed too early. Of those years, 1885 was a particularly good one, his best since 1877, and was regarded at the time as marking something of a revival. Yet the *annus mirabilis* of 1895 was still ten years away.

If in 1878 W. G. had devoted himself to the repelling of the Australians, he was on the whole successful. Only in one year did the invaders have the best of England, but that one tragic year, 1881, will be remembered when all the English victories are forgotten. The story of it has been told over and over again, and as to some of its events, as in the case of Cobden's over, scarcely anybody can now be sure whether they are mythical or not. Was C. T. Studd really so paralysed with nervousness before his last innings that he walked up and down and round and round the pavilion wrapped in a blanket? Did Peate really say, on being remonstrated for hitting recklessly, 'You see, sir, I couldn't trust Mr. Studd'? At any rate we know the bare scores, and they are

65

*This fine portrait of W. G. Grace in the 1880s, which hangs at Lords, gives a vivid impression of the masterful cricketer's awesome appearance.*

enough. Australia lost their first six wickets for 30, and were all out for 64. England, with W. G. yorked by Spofforth for 4, made only 102, and thus signally failed to rub in a glorious chance. Next day, after a heavy night's rain on a sodden and muddy wicket, Massie attacked terrifically, and Bannerman was like a rock. Yet Australia were all out for 122 – only 84 runs on. Barlow went down and Hornby went down, but Ulyett and W. G. added 36. The worst was, humanly speaking, over when Ulyett was caught at the wicket, and, soon after, W. G. was caught at mid-off for 32. He said afterwards, 'Well, well, I left six men to get thirty odd runs and they could not get them,' and, as he said it, he is alleged to have looked for once almost depressed. Spofforth took, in all, fourteen wickets for 90 runs, and a gentleman in the *Sporting Times* made his joke about the Ashes, of which we have since had more than sufficient time to grow tired.

Outraged honour was reasonably satisfied in 1884, when England, having been saved by Shrewsbury at Old Trafford, won at Lord's, and made a draw of it at the Oval. It is one of the memorable details of this last match that W. G. kept wicket while Alfred Lyttelton bowled lobs; another is that Scotton took nearly six hours to make his 90 runs. When it is remembered that he was left-handed, we may well think that dreariness must have reached

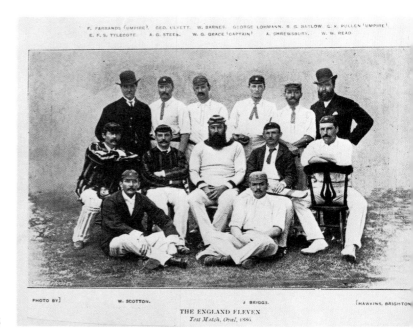

F. FARRANDS (UMPIRE). GEO. ULYETT. W. BARNES. GEORGE LOHMANN. R. G. BARLOW. G. K. PULLEN (UMPIRE).
E. F. S. TYLECOTE. A. G. STEEL. W. G. GRACE (CAPTAIN). A. SHREWSBURY. W. W. READ.

PHOTO BY]        W. SCOTTON.        J. BRIGGS.        [HAWKINS, BRIGHTON

THE ENGLAND ELEVEN
*Test Match, Oval, 1886.*

*The doctor's winning team of 1886*

its ultimate point. In 1886, England won very easily against a team that was thoroughly disappointing. W. G.'s 170 in the first match has been mentioned. His comment, that 'the poor Australians did not have much of a show with us in this match,' understates the case. They had another, though less severe, dose of Scotton, as well as of W. G., and then Lohmann and Briggs routed them twice. In 1888, Turner and Ferris bowled continuously, heroically, and magnificently, and won one Test Match, but they could not pull their weak batting side through in the other two, both of which England won easily.

With the 'nineties we come to the last ten years, not of W. G.'s cricketing life, but of the longest and most splendid phase of it. In the 'sixties, when still in his teens, he had begun to play first for England. At the end of the 'nineties, when he was fifty, he played for England for the last time. After the first Test Match in 1899, he was not chosen to play in the second; that was the end of the things that could never happen again.

There were, however, wonderful things to be recorded before that, and the last great decade began with a great adventure. In the winter of 1891, W. G. revisited Australia, as captain of Lord Sheffield's team, after an interval of eighteen years. It was a hard enterprise for a man of his weight and girth to undertake in his

*Dr. W. G. Grace makes a formidable image in the Illustrated London News of 1888, where he was featured as 'Man of the Day'.*

*Alfred Bryan's caricature of Grace at Lords, 1890.*

ALFRED SHAW.    A. E. STODDART.    M. READ.    H. P. PHILIPSON.    O. G. RADCLIFFE.

ABEL.   LOHMANN.   G. MACGREGOR.   BRIGGS.   PEEL.   W. G. GRACE.   ATTEWELL.   BEAN.   SHARPE.

LORD SHEFFIELD'S AUSTRALIAN TEAM, 1891-2.
[*Photograph taken in the Botanical Gardens, Adelaide.*]

*The doctor and his men arrive at Adelaide, 1891.*

forty-fourth year, but he received a fee of £3,000 and all his expenses, and he entirely justified himself. He played in very nearly every match, and headed the averages both in the eleven a side matches and in those against odds. In his own writings he had nothing but grateful things to say, and no doubt in retrospect he thought he had enjoyed the tour; perhaps, on the whole, he had, for nothing could damp his cheerful spirit or make him cross for long. That there were moments when he was cross, admits of no doubt, for on three occasions the old umpiring trouble broke out again. There was one long wrangle – and W. G. could wrangle when he had a mind to it – over who should be the English umpire against New South Wales; there was another about a certain catch, when the umpire did not like being criticised; there was a third, about whether or not the wicket was fit for play, and this led to some talk of his taking the English team off the field. These things probably sound more unpleasant than they really were. It is to be remembered that while W. G. always wanted his pound of flesh, he bore no malice when he did not get it, and that he had not the particular kind of sensitiveness that shrinks from an argument. The tour was, on the whole, a success, and the still surpassing greatness of W. G. could still be measured by the surpassing greatness of the noise that announced the fall of his wicket.

# 7
# 1892-1895

THE success in Australia had been all the more welcome because it had followed a really dismal summer for W. G. – a strained knee, only something over twenty innings and an average of 19, the lowest he had ever had in first-class cricket. Naturally the more depressing prophets had said that this visit to Australia would be one more instance of the pitcher going too often to the well. 1892 was better, with an average of 30; in 1893 it was 35; and in 1894 it was just below 30, and for beloved Gloucestershire it was below 20. There were in that year some fine scores for other teams, notably two hundreds against Cambridge – 139 at Fenner's, and 196 at Lord's. Yet there was something of bitterness to mar both those big scores, for in those matches W. G.'s eldest son, W. G. Junr., failed, and his father was desperately and pathetically anxious that he should get his blue. The younger W. G. had done well for the Clifton eleven, and if a somewhat angular, ungainly, and artificial batsman, yet he could get runs, and all that affectionate encouragement could do for him had doubtless been done. For once the writer can here speak from direct personal experience, as he bowled at him, and, what is more, got him out in a Long Vacation match between Trinity and Pembroke – the last man he ever did get out except small boys in a 'fathers' match'. It was not an experience to heighten one's admiration for his batting, which

69

*Like many sons of famous fathers, W. G. Grace junior could not avoid following in some of his father's footsteps, although he presented a very different image to the world.*

seemed a little lacking in natural dash, due no doubt to the fact that he had broken an arm as a boy and it had remained stiff ever afterwards.

In that first match at Fenner's, W. G. took his boy in with him, and the boy was caught at the wicket for a duck and had no second innings. At Lord's, when he went in later, the very same fate befell him. Here he had a second innings, and made 50 off the tired Cambridge bowlers, whom his father had already pounded metaphorically into a jelly, but there was to be no blue that year.

However, it came next year, when young W. G. went in first for Cambridge and played two sound innings, and his father burst upon the world for the first time in history in a vast frock-coat and a tall hat which seemed to shine with the reflected joy and glory of its owner. With that blue came the thousand runs in May, the hundredth hundred, and the national testimonial, and it probably gave more unalloyed pleasure than all the rest of these wonderful things put together. 1895 was, as W. G. himself wrote, the 'crowning point of his cricketing career'; a second blooming, an occasion on which all the enthusiasm and affection of the cricket lovers in England could find an unrestrained vent. In England we are always kind and indulgent to our players of games that are not so young as they once were; we never think, unless we are absolutely driven to it, that they lag superfluous on the stage; we may cry out for youth to have its chance, but we cheer age the loudest and on the smallest provocation. And here was a chance to cheer on a provocation that no man, young or old, had ever been able to give before. The years had rolled away, and, for this one year, W. G. once more stood supreme as in the 'seventies, a champion not of the storied past but of the living present, the unbeatable, the unbowlable, the killer of bowlers, who never tired nor relented, but slew and slew and slew. It was as if by means of some magic time-machine the new generation could see him just as their fathers had done.

True to his custom, W. G. had begun practising in the bleak winds of March, and by April he had shown that his eye was in by finding his way through twenty-two colts in the field for a score of 101. May came in fine and warm, a month of hard wickets and sunshine to loosen middle-aged backs. The first eight days of the month were wasted, but on the ninth he took the field for M.C.C. against Sussex, and in the first innings he was caught by 'Ranji' for 13. The same fate ought to have overtaken him in the second, for, when he had made only one more than the unlucky number, that usually lethal fielder missed him, and W. G., chaffing him between the overs, went on to make 103, at the end of which a very mild Nemesis caused him to be caught off Ranji's bowling.

It was Mr. George Brann who caught him, from a monstrous ballooning hit in which W. G. suddenly indulged, and he has told me an interesting thing about the match. Although it was W. G.'s first first-class match of the season, rumours were already abroad that the 'Old Man' was in great form, that he had drunk of some elixir, and was playing once more as he had done in his youth. So there was immense curiosity to see him, and Mr. Brann says that, from the moment W. G. came in, he realised that this was a batsman he had never seen before. He had been playing with and against W. G. since the early 'eighties: he had seen him make many runs, but here, from the first ball bowled, was something different,

*W.G. with J. M. Blackham, captain of the Australian Touring Team of 1893. Engraving by Alfred Bryan.*

*W.G., at the time of his greatest glory, both dominated and symbolized the game.*

a complete lack of stiffness, an utterly free and confident wrist play. This was the real thing, and Mr. Brann for the first time appreciated to the full what the bowlers of the 'seventies had had to endure.

W. G. only wanted one more hundred for his century of centuries, but this was not to be in the Yorkshire match, for he only made 18 and 25. Half the month of May had sped, and he had only made 159 out of the 1,000 that was to be. The scene changes to

Bristol – Gloucester against Somerset – and now he set to work in earnest. Mr. C. L. Townsend, who, then little more than a boy, made a big stand with him, has recorded that W. G. betrayed a very human anxiety. 'This,' he writes in the *Memorial Biography*, 'was the one and only time I ever saw him flustered, namely when the last runs were needed for his hundredth hundred. Poor Sam Woods could hardly bowl the ball and the Doctor was nearly as bad.' However, the momentous runs came at last; no one then dreamed of an impious Hobbs, and the wonder that could never be repeated had come to pass. Immediately the crisis had passed, W. G. was himself again, and, with a cheerful venom and an insatiable rejoicing in his own strength, went on to flog the Somerset bowling till the second hundred loomed near. It came, and with it a magnum of champagne to be drunk on the field, but even that had no melting influence. 'The Fates,' he wrote, 'apparently decreed that there should be no mistake about it, for my score was 288.' Never did the Fates have a more loyal adjutant; he was probably rather disappointed that the third hundred escaped him. Not so the Somerset bowlers. It is even rumoured that they thought the Doctor might have been a little more lenient, since they had done their best for his first hundred.

*W.G. was not a man to let a special event go by uncelebrated. In 1895, when he had scored his hundredth century, he arranged a private dinner party, and had eighteen plates made by Coalport china, engraved with his signature in the centre, encircled by the details of his hundred centuries. The manufacturers gained Grace's permission to sell copies of this plate with a portrait of the master in the centre instead of the signature, as illustrated here. In later years Colin Cowdrey celebrated his hundredth hundred in a similar way, and the tradition is now carried on with commemorative plates for John Edrich and Geoff Boycott.*

*The Paddington train in the 1890s. The station master was used to holding up the train for Dr. Grace who must have been one of its best customers on his journeys to and from Bristol.*

For the Gentlemen, at Cambridge, he made 52, and then to Gravesend, where Kent were beaten after a match that deserves recording for its own sake. Kent went in first, and made 470. Gloucestershire replied with 443 – W. G. 257, and last man out. Kent went in again, and, for no accountable reason save that they were liquid lead and wedges in the hands of Fate, were tumbled out by Roberts and Painter for the ridiculous amount of 76. Gloucestershire, wanting 106 to win, made the runs for the loss of one wicket – W. G. not out 73. He had been in the field, either batting or fielding, throughout the entire three days' play; he had bowled too, and taken a wicket in Kent's first innings. And he was nearly forty-seven and weighed untold stone.

Playing for England against Surrey, in Walter Read's benefit match, he was bowled by Richardson for 18, and there was no second chance. So, by this time, May had almost run its course. There remained only the first two days of Gloucestershire and Middlesex at Lord's, May 30th and 31st, and 153 runs were still wanting to make up the thousand. Gloucester won the toss, and W. G. started carefully and methodically on his task – only 58 by lunch-time, and a slow bowler, whom he could not 'get at' so quickly as of old, bothering him. Gradually he became fiercer and more confident; the hundred was safely passed, and the desired figure drew nearer and nearer while Lord's held its breath. At 149, the slow bowler aforesaid, E. A. Nepean, mercifully put an end to the universal agony with a long hop to leg. There was no tragedy,

*Stuart Wortley's famous painting of W. G. Grace at the wicket in 1890. The original is a Lord's*

no mis-hit, no lurking fieldsman; the deed was done. Sixteen more runs were added, and then he was bowled for 169. The sound of the cheering in front of the pavilion has scarcely died away yet. If only the old lady in the red cloak could have been there to hear it!

This sort of thing could not go on for ever, or at any rate not on quite so terrific a scale, and there came a spell of wet wickets during which W. G., in his own words, 'was no longer master of the situation,' but there were other great innings before the season ended. It was like old times to see him make yet another hundred against the Players at Lord's – a thing he had not done since 1876. The Kent bowlers were mercilessly dealt with at Lord's, as if they had not had enough at Gravesend: the Jubilee match of the I Zingari against the Gentlemen of England produced 101, to win the match for the Gentlemen in an hour and three-quarters, with two big hits to end with, just when it seemed that the hundred would escape him. By the end of the year, W. G. had made 2,346 runs, with nine centuries.

The wave of enthusiasm, which swept cricketers off their legs all over the country, produced delightfully practical results, for there followed a wave of testimonials. The proprietors of the *Daily Telegraph* started a national shilling testimonial, which produced more than £5,000. The *Sportsman* collected another fund, and handed over the proceeds to a third founded by the Committee of the M.C.C. Gloucestershire had a fourth fund of its own, and, in the end, W. G. retired to his winter quarters the richer by an honest pot of money, £9,073 8s. 3d.

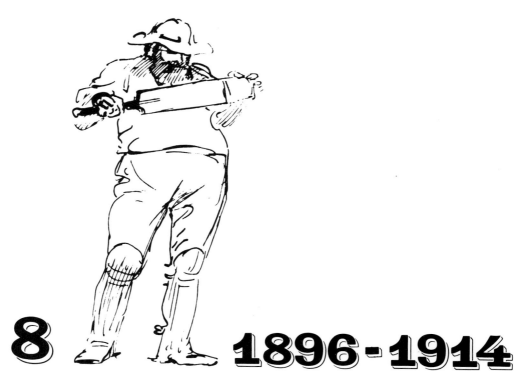

# 8 1896-1914

AFTER that culminating year everything in W. G.'s life, as far as pure cricket is concerned, must appear, in retrospect, an anticlimax. Yet, at the time, his sun, if it were setting, seemed to be doing so very slowly, and when the end came at long last, it was 'a sundown splendid and serene.' 1896 saw as small a falling off as was humanly possible; indeed it was far better than many earlier years, and he ended fifth in the averages, with an aggregate of over 2,000 runs. There was not yet the faintest doubt of his place in an England eleven against Australia, and he had the satisfaction of making a valuable small score in the deciding Test Match at the Oval, and then of seeing Peel and Hearne rout the Australians in the fourth innings and win the rubber. They went in to get 111 to win, and lost seven wickets for 14. McKibbin hit about with desperate heroism, but the last wicket fell at 44. Peel had bowled magnificently.

It was in this year that Ernest Jones, the Australian fast bowler, made himself immortal by bowling through the immortal beard. Here I find myself in a difficulty, for the *Memorial Biography* says that it happened in the first Test Match at Lord's, and Lord Harris declared that he saw the incident. On the other hand, Sir Stanley Jackson is positive that it was in the opening match of the tour against Lord Sheffield's Eleven. He played in both matches, and

*The England team for the final T[...] Match at the Oval in 1896. Prin[...] Ranjitsinhji is on Grace's right, F. S. Jackson on his left. J. T. Hearne is on the right of the back row, and R. Peel is cross-legged, right.*

with that I shall not enter the field of historical controversy but tell the story as he has told it to me. Jones was bowling with inconceivable 'go' and pace; his run up to the wicket and the swing of his mighty arm were terrific, and the wicket was bumpy. The first ball was a short one, it brushed W. G.'s beard, went over the wicket-keeper's head, and, with as it seemed but another bound, was against the screen. W. G. came a little way up the pitch, calling out 'What's this? What's this?' or, according to another account, 'Whatever are ye at?' Trott said quietly, 'Steady, Jonah, steady,' and Jones, most good-natured of men, made his often-quoted apology, 'Sorry, Doctor, she slipped.'

It is at any rate certain that the wicket in the match was alarmingly fiery, and that W. G. had on his body, close to his heart, marks blue, black, and red where Jones had hit him. He exhibited them to his friends when he got back to Bristol, and his comment is worth quoting again, 'Well, he did rap me a bit sharp.' Incidentally Jones also 'rapped' F. S. Jackson in the ribs to the extent of cracking one of them, but the batsman declared that it was his own fault and not the bowler's.

The next was a year of marking-time for his Jubilee (over 1,500 runs nevertheless, and an average of just under 40), and then the great popularity began to surge and thunder again as, in 1898,

*One of the twenty-two silver med[...] cast to celebrate W.G.'s ha[...] century, on July 18th, 18[...]*

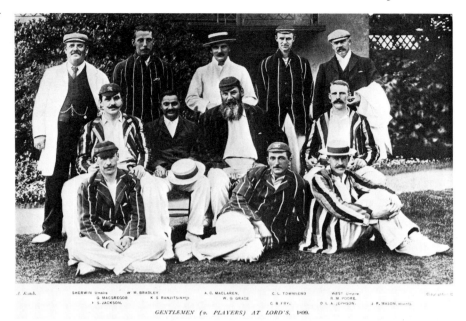

*e Gentlemen of 1899. In front of W. G. Grace sits C. B. Fry.*

J. Kidd.
SHERWIN Umpire    W. M. BRADLEY    A. C. MACLAREN.    C. L. TOWNSEND    WEST Umpire    Copyright C
G. MACGREGOR    K S RANJITSINHJI    W G GRACE    R. M. POORE.
F. S. JACKSON.    C. B. FRY.    D. L. A. JEPHSON.    J. R. MASON. Scorer.

*GENTLEMEN (v. PLAYERS) AT LORD'S. 1899.*

W. G. reached his fiftieth year. Gentlemen and Players was chosen for his birthday match, at Lord's; the sides were worthy of the occasion, and those who played were given a special medal. W. G. was lame, and had a bruised hand into the bargain, but he got a much-needed wicket when the Players went in. He opened the Gentlemen's innings on the second day, and afforded the big crowd an hour and a half's pure hero-worship before he was caught at the wicket for 43. Yet the greatest moment was to come. On the last day, the Gentlemen went in to make 296 in less than three hours. W. G., owing to his hand and his lameness, kept himself back, and J. T. Hearne sent the Gentlemen to the right-about so quickly that seven wickets were down for 77. Then at last the giant bestirred himself and went in, *spes ultima* of his side. Two more wickets fell for three runs: Kortright joined his captain, and Hearne and Lockwood and Haigh were defied. On crept the clock till there were but four minutes left, and, at last, Kortright was caught, high up at coverpoint. Could he have left that ball alone? I know not, but I wish those gallant two could have made a draw of it. As it was, W. G. took out his bat, undefeated by the enemies that he had held so long in subjection. There was a banquet in the evening, and W. G. made a rather longer speech than usual, but not a very long one. Even in that festive hour the old will to victory

79

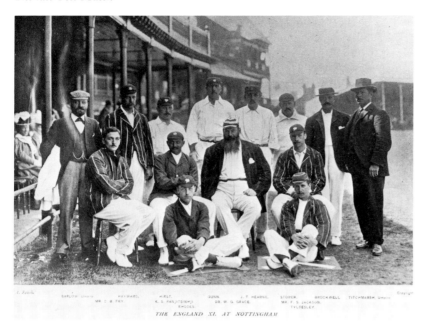

THE ENGLAND XI. AT NOTTINGHAM

*The England Eleven for the first Test at Nottingham, 1899, W.G.'s last Test Match.*

survived, and, unfulfilled, brought with it not bitterness indeed but regrets; if the Players had not won the toss, he declared, they would have been beaten men that night. Can any birthday be quite perfect?

1899 was a year of landmarks; W. G.'s last Test Match, and his last match for Gloucestershire. About the first, there was no true cause for lamentation, and W. G. himself felt neither soreness nor sadness. 'Never mind,' had said the prize-giver at some sports in which W. G. had swept the board thirty years before, 'Never mind, he'll grow old and stiff some day.' The day had been long postponed, but at last it had dawned, as it must for any player of any game. It was a different matter with Gloucestershire. He could still have played for his county for several years to come, and his last match for it ought to have ended in a blaze of autumn sunshine, and a 'Hail and Farewell'. As it was, it ended abruptly in the early summer, with no good-bye, in resentment and misunderstanding.

This was an Australians' year, and W. G. took them seriously. As one of those who played for England with him has said, he always pulled at his old beard when he played against them. This year, for the first time, he half wanted to play against them, and half did not want to. He had grown very, very heavy, and had begun to feel that he was no longer up to it. In many ways he would have

*'As we went down the pavilion steps, he looked extremely cheerful, and brushing his beard aside as though he meant business he said, "Look here,*

*The end of the first day's play*

*Charlie Fry, remember I'm not a
printer, like you." Anyhow, we went
in and put up a very good stand – I
think it was 75 before W.G. got out.'*
C. B. FRY

liked to get out, and yet he could not quite drag himself out; he had
played so long, cricket had been so much his life; there was
something that prevented him from saying the decisive words,
perhaps from thinking the decisive thoughts. And so he played in
the first Test Match at Nottingham. He made eight and twenty
runs, and England did not lose, but there was a feeling abroad, of
which he was conscious, that the time for departure had come. He
could not get to the ball very well in the field, and a small section of
the crowd expressed themselves audibly on this point. It was the
first and only time such a thing had ever happened, and it must
have hurt. As he travelled home in the train, he said to one who
was, after an interval, to succeed him as captain, 'It's all over,
Jacker; I shan't play again.'

For the second match he was not chosen, but G. L. Jessop
played, in his stead, his first match for England, so that
Gloucestershire to Gloucestershire succeeded. Again W. G.
pulled at his beard, and said, 'Not good enough – but I'm not done
yet.' He would have been glad then to have gone earlier, before
there could have been any question, but, as it was, he accepted the
situation with perfect naturalness, modesty, and good humour,
and he certainly was not done yet, for he made 50 off Jones at his
fastest for the M.C.C. against the Australians, and he was run out

*Pencil sketch of W. G. Grace at Crystal Palace, by H. S. Tuke, R.A.*

when within sight of yet another hundred against the Players.

For Gloucestershire he played last in the early summer against Middlesex, and then vanished suddenly in a maze of contradictory statements and rumours. It is likely enough that he and the county authorities had not been in perfect agreement for some time, for W. G. was always a one-man selection committee, and it had been suggested that there should be a more numerous and orthodox one. The real trouble arose, however, when W. G. accepted the management of the London County team at the Crystal Palace, and proposed at the same time to retain the captaincy of Gloucestershire. This did not seem a feasible plan: the county authorities said so, and that was the end. One may sympathise with both parties, and it was natural enough at the time that W. G. should feel acutely such a parting from a side which he and his brothers had made. In the end, however, no malice was borne;

Gloucestershire is the county of the Graces as long as there is any cricket, and that is enough.

The next eight years may be dealt with briefly. They were far from barren ones either in point of runs or amusement, but all things are comparative, and the great times were now definitely over. For five years W. G. was the mainspring of the London County side at the Crystal Palace, and got plenty of fun out of its

*W.G. with some of the players from London County Club at Crystal Palace, and,* BELOW *putting on his pads at Lords.*

matches, especially when he had his old friend Murdoch to contribute to it, but the venture was never really a success.

He played some fine innings, both for that side and others. In 1900 he made 126 in South *v.* North at Lord's against a galaxy of northern bowling, and it was like old days to find him at his best in a benefit match. He also made two hundreds, one against Worcestershire and one against M.C.C., for London County. In 1901 he again made a hundred against the M.C.C., and two innings of over 50 for the Gentlemen, one at the Oval and one at Hastings. What was more remarkable, he did two really fine pieces of bowling at Lord's against the M.C.C. – 7 for 30, and 6 for 80. In 1902 he had five of the Australian wickets for 29, and made 82 for the Gentlemen at the Oval, and yet another hundred against the M.C.C. In 1903, London County played Gloucestershire, and his old side felt the full weight of his arm – 150 runs and six wickets for 82. His fifty-sixth birthday – in 1904 – was celebrated by an innings of 166 against the M.C.C., and his last first-class match for the M.C.C. at Lord's saw him make 27 against Kotze's fast bowling for the South Africans.

In 1905 the London County experiment had ended, and he had fewer opportunities, but he made at least one good score, 71 against Oxford, and then, in 1906, came what was almost the end. He was

*W.G. with W. L. Murdoch playing for the London County against Warwickshire in 1904, a few days before his 56th birthday.*

now fifty-eight, and Mr. Leveson-Gower asked him to play once again for the Gentlemen at the Oval.

'Yes, Snipe,' he said. 'Yes – I'll do it.' 'And what if you fail?' he was asked, and he answered, 'I've been well advertised all my life. If I fail it'll be passed over, but if I do well it'll be a great exit.'

And a supremely great exit it was. Once again his birthday had come round, and, forty-one years after he had first played for the Gentlemen, he made 74 runs. Then, tired but happy, he lumbered into the pavilion, threw his bat on the table, and said, 'I shan't play any more.'

He never did play any more against the Players, but in 1907 he played for the Gentlemen against Surrey, the opening match of the season, and in 1908 he played in the same match on an April day of

*In his old age W.G. was often asked to play at Shillinglee Park, Sussex, the temporary home of Prince Ranjitsinhji. This photograph was taken in 1908.*

*On June 10th, 1911, W.G. played for Prince Albert of Schleswig-Holstein's XI against Charterhouse at Cumberland Lodge. He made a duck. The dapper young man wearing a boater photographed here with the king of cricket is Edward, Prince of Wales.*

*W.G. photographed at Eltham before his last match in 1914. Standing third from the right is his youngest son, C. B. Grace.*

snow-showers. He made 15 and 25, and bowled twelve balls for five runs and no wicket. That was the end of his first-class cricket. He played afterwards in a number of minor matches for the M.C.C., and for local sides, and his very last match of all was a few days before the beginning of the war, for Eltham against Grove Park on July 25th, 1914. He made 31 runs on a fiery and impossible wicket, and the last bowlers who ever bowled to him could not get him out.

'W. G.,' said an old friend of his, 'was just a great big schoolboy in everything he did.' It would be difficult in a single sentence to come nearer to the clue to his character. He had all the schoolboy's love for elementary and boisterous jokes: his distaste for learning; his desperate and undisguised keenness; his guilelessness and his guile; his occasional pettishness and pettiness; his endless power of recovering his good spirits. To them may be added two qualities not as a rule to be found in schoolboys; a wonderful modesty and lack of vanity; an invariable kindness to those younger than himself, 'except,' as one of his most devoted friends has observed, 'that he tried to chisel them out l.b.w.'

If one had to choose a single epithet to describe him, it would, I think, be simple. 'I am not a psychologist,' he says in one of his books, and his estimate was doubtless accurate. He did not think very deeply or very subtly about anybody or anything; perhaps not even about cricket, although his knowledge of it was intuitively profound, his judgment of a cricketer unique. Of all the stories about him none is better known than his answer to a question as to how a particular stroke should be made: 'You put the bat against the ball.' It may be read in one of two slightly different senses, and in either it seems to reveal something of his character. Take it as a serious attempt to explain the whole secret of a stroke, an earnest endeavour to help the learner, and in that sense it shows his essential simplicity. Again it may be taken as a reflection on those who want to be too clever and abstruse, and I imagine that W. G. did not want people to be clever. He was too modest to have the contemptuous arrogance of the unlearned towards learning; that belongs to the lout, and he had no trace of it, but for his own part he liked best the other simple folk like himself. His interests were all of the open air. If people wanted to read books, no doubt they got pleasure from it, but it was a pleasure that he could not really understand. Wisden, yes, perhaps, to confirm a memory or refute an argument, or in winter as an earnest of the summer to come; but in a general way books were bad for cricket. 'How can you expect to make runs,' he said to one of the Gloucestershire side, 'when you are always reading?'; and added, almost gratuitously, 'You don't catch me that way.' I have searched in vain for anyone who ever saw him take the risk, except in the case of a newspaper or a medical book in which he wanted to look up a point.

W. G. was not an intellectual man, and even as regards his own subject his was not an analytical brain, but by instinct or genius – call it what you will – he could form a judgement of a cricketer to which all others bowed. One who played much with him has given me two instances to which many more might, of course, be added. A schoolboy who had made innumerable runs for his school, and was generally regarded as an extraordinary cricketer, played in his first first-class match with W. G., and made a respectable score. Everybody crowded round the oracle to hear the verdict, and expected a favourable one. 'He'll never make a first-class cricketer' – that was all, and it turned out to be entirely true. Here is a converse example. When Mr. Jessop first appeared for Gloucestershire, those who now realise that they ought to have known better were struck only by the more rough-hewn and bucolic aspects of his batting. 'What have you got here, old man?' they asked W. G. rather disparagingly. 'Ah, you wait and see what I've got here,' he answered with a touch of truculence, and went on to say that in a year or so this would be the finest hitter that had ever been seen. That this verdict also turned out true is hardly worth the saying.

Moreover, if W. G. did not possess what is generally called cleverness, he had, within certain precise limits, a remarkable acuteness. He might not think deeply, but on his own subjects he could think quickly. 'A man must get up very early in the morning,' said the Game Chicken, 'to get the best of John Gully,' and many a cricketer might well have said it of W. G. He had that sort of quickness of apprehension that may, without disrespect, perhaps be called cunning, and is often to be found, a little surprisingly, in those who seem at first sight simple-minded and almost rustic. He had plenty of shrewdness too in judging the qualities of men, so far as they interested him and came within his sphere. He might occasionally do ill-judged things in the excitement of the moment, but at the bottom of everything there was a good hard kernel of common sense.

We are told that when W. G. first appeared in first-class cricket he was shy, and we can picture him a tall, gawky, uneasy boy. He had not been to a public school; he came from a small country doctor's family; he had met few people except in his own country neighbourhood, and he suddenly found himself among those who had had a different sort of up-bringing. It is no wonder that he was silent and uncomfortable; but fame and popularity are wonderful softeners of that agony of shyness, and, if he perhaps kept a little of it deep down inside him, there was no external trace of it. He was perfectly natural with all whom he met, and if he liked them he was soon friendly and hearty with them. He was helped by a wonderful unselfconsciousness. He seemed to take himself for granted, at once a supreme player of his game, and, off the field, as an ordinary person, and did not bother his head about what impression he made. He was far better known by sight than any man in England. Long after his cricketing days were over, he had only to pass through a village street in a motor-car for windows to be thrown up and fingers to be pointed, but he seemed, and really was, as nearly as possible unaware of it, unless perhaps his admirer was a small child, to whom he liked to wave his hand. This un-selfconsciousness pervaded his whole existence. He had come, as has been said, from a home comparatively countrified and uncultivated; he kept, to some extent at least, its manners and its way of speech all his life. He mixed constantly with those who were, in a snobbish sense, his superiors and had other ways and other manners, and I do not believe that he ever gave such things a thought. He recognised different standards in the houses he stayed at, to the extent that there were some to which he ought to take his 'dancing-pumps,' and that was all. He liked friendliness and cheerfulness wherever he met it; he was ready to give it himself, and never thought of anything else that could be demanded of him.

I do not know if I am right, but he gave me the impression that the one thing that would not go down with him was any

The "G.O.M."

*Rip's caricature of W.G.*

elaborateness of manner, any too formal politeness. I remember a little scene on a golf course. I was playing with him in a foursome, and someone unintentionally drove into us from behind. W. G., always jealous of his rights in any game, resented it, but the driver of the ball apologised with extreme politeness, and surely all would now be over. But it was not; the more careful the apologies the less did W. G. let the poor man alone, until he made the rest of the foursome feel very uncomfortable. I thought then, and I think now, that if the offender had come up, and said cheerfully, 'Doctor, I'm awfully sorry,' and had even clapped him on the back, all would have been well, but he was of the sort that cannot for the life of them clap people on the back, and nothing could atone.

It has been said that W. G. liked simple jokes, and if they were familiar ones of the 'old grouse in the gun-room type' so much the better. There seems to me something extremely characteristic about a story, very small and mild in itself, told by Mr. C. E. Green in the *Memorial Biography*. Mr. Green was Master of the Essex Hounds, and had the hounds brought for W. G. to look at after breakfast. He liked the hounds, and he liked the Master's big grey horse, and, Mr. Green goes on, 'For years afterwards whenever we met he would sing out "How's my old grey horse?"' That is perhaps hardly worthy of the name of joke, but, whatever it was, it was the kind of friendly chaff that pleased W. G. He liked jokes to do with conviviality, for he was a convivial soul. Essentially temperate in his everyday private life, he enjoyed good things on anything in the nature of an occasion; he had, as I fancy, a kind of Dickensian relish for good cheer, not merely the actual enjoyment of it but also the enjoyment of thinking and talking about it, and he combined with this, of course, a much greater practical capacity than Dickens ever had. A whole bottle of champagne was a mere nothing to him; having consumed it he would go down on all fours, and balance the bottle on the top of his head and rise to his feet again. Nothing could disturb that magnificent constitution, and those who hoped by a long and late sitting to shorten his innings next day often found themselves disappointed. His regular habit while cricketing was to drink one large whisky and soda, with a touch of angostura bitters, at lunch, and another when the day's play ended; this allowance he never varied or exceeded till the evening came, and, despite his huge frame, though he never dieted, he ate sparingly. His one attempt at a weight-reducing regimen was the drinking of cider. As he believed in a moderate amount of good drink, so he disbelieved strongly in tobacco. He had been brought up in a non-

'The labours of 'Arry'. A Punch cartoon of 1895 by Phil May which caught the eye of W.G.

smoking family (though his brother Alfred became a backslider), and stuck to its tenets religiously all his life. It was an aphorism of his that 'you can get rid of drink, but you can never get rid of smoke.' He constantly proclaimed it as his own private belief, but he never made any attempt to put his team on any allowance of tobacco.

Mr. A. J. Webbe tells me that he remembers at his mother's house in Eaton Square, W. G. marching round the drawing-room after dinner, bearing the coal-scuttle on his head as a helmet, with the poker carried as a sword. It is an agreeable picture, and we may feel sure that W. G. was ready to go on marching just a little longer than anyone else, for his energy was as inexhaustible as his humour was childlike; he must be playing at something – billiards or cards, dancing or coal-scuttles, anything but sitting down. The simplicity of his humour often took, naturally enough, a practical direction; in one corner of his mind there probably lurked all his life amiable thoughts of booby traps and apple-pie beds, and he was even known in an exuberant moment on a golfing expedition to hurl rocks at a boat like another Polyphemus.

He carried his practical joking into the realms of cricket, as when, according to a well-known story, he caused the batsman to look up at the sky to see some imaginary birds, with the result that

WEST HALL COPSE,
WAPLINGHAM
SURREY

27 Nov. 1895

Dear Sir,

Why — oh Why — did you give 'Square leg' wicket keeper gloves when you showed us 'Arry' at the wicket? My Sons who are Cricketers also demanded an explanation of me last Evening at dinner

Oh — said I — to counteract Arry's evident violent play. But they were not satisfied & still wanted to know why some of the spectators were wearing overcoats. 'For the same reason' said I.

Yours truly

W. G. Grace

Phil May Esq

*.G. wrote this letter to the ~~cartoonist~~rtoonist. Phil May's reply was : 'To keep his hands warm.'*

the poor innocent was blinded by the sun and promptly bowled. With this we come to one of the most difficult questions about W. G.: did he at all, and, if so, how far, overstep the line which, in a game, divides fair play from sharp practice? There is one preliminary thing to say, namely that there is no absolute standard in these matters, and that standards differ with times and societies. The sportsmen of the early nineteenth century did, naturally and unblushingly, things that would be considered very unsportsmanlike nowadays. In those days everything was a 'match': each party must look after himself; it was play or pay, and the devil take the hindermost. Anybody who reads the autobiography of the Squire, George Osbaldeston, will get an insight into the sporting morals of that day. 'A noble fellow, always straight,' said Mr. Budd of the Squire: but he deliberately pulled a horse in order to get the better of those who in his estimation had over-reached him, and, generally speaking, it was one of his guiding principles in all sports not to let the cat out of the bag. He never did what he thought a dishonourable thing, but he had a different standard of honour from our own. I believe that in W. G. was found something of a survival of this older tradition. He had his own notions of what was right and permissible, and I am convinced that he would never willingly have done anything contrary to them; the difficulty arose when other people did not think something permissible and he did. He would never have dreamed of purposely getting in the way of a fieldsman who might otherwise have caught him, but to shout cheerfully to that fieldsman, 'Miss it,' was – at any rate in a certain class of cricket – not merely within the law, but rather a good joke.

The law was the law, though in his intense keenness he could not wholly rid himself of the idea that it was sometimes unjustly enforced against him; what the law allowed was allowable. It was always worth appealing; if the umpire thought a man was out l.b.w., it did not matter what the bowler thought. 'You weren't out, you know,' he was sometimes heard to say to a retiring batsman against whom he had appealed, and thought no shame to do so: everything was open and above board; if the umpire decided you were out – and he sometimes decided wrong – that was all about it. He wanted desperately to get the other side out, and any fair way of doing so was justifiable; he never stooped to what he thought was a mean way. No man knew the law better, and it could seldom be said against him that he was wrong, but rather that he was too desperately right. Sometimes the fact that he had the reputation of wanting his pound of flesh caused him to be unjustly criticised when his claim was an entirely proper one. There was a certain match between Gloucestershire and Sussex, in which, at the end of the second innings of Sussex, the Sussex total for two innings was exactly equal to that of Gloucestershire's one innings, and there were left some eleven or eleven and a half minutes of time. Ten minutes' interval left a minute or so in which to get the one run for a ten-wicket victory. W. G. properly declared that Gloucestershire should go in. Sussex to some extent seem to have demurred on the ground that there was not time for an over. However, they went out to field. Ranji had changed into ordinary clothes, and W. G. went out to field as substitute for him. Tate bowled the one over to Jessop, and nothing could be done with three balls. The fourth was pushed gently towards W. G. at point, and the run gained almost before he had had time to stoop. It is a subject for irreverent speculation what would have happened if the batsmen had been caught in two minds in the middle of the pitch. Would that ball have gone straight to the wicket keeper or is it possible that there would have been an overthrow?

In the matter of enforcing rules – and on this particular occasion W. G. was clearly in the right – the manner of his bringing up ought always to be remembered. His early cricket had been played with a father and three elder brothers who were going to stand no

nonsense from the younger ones. The boy was taught to behave himself, and this meant, amongst other things, to stick to the rules. It was natural enough that when he grew older he expected other players to behave themselves too. It may be said that he did not sufficiently distinguish between big points and small ones, but the answer is that, where cricket was concerned, there was for W. G. no such thing as a small point. It might seem trivial to more easy-going or more flexibly minded persons; never to him; and if things were not, as he thought, just right, he came out bluntly and impetuously with his opinion.

His elder brothers had not had any excessive consideration for his young feelings, and it may be that, on the field of play, he had not a great deal of consideration for other people's. No doubt W. G. at point could be a little trying to the highly strung batsman. 'These Graces chatter so,' said Sir Timothy O'Brien, who did not suffer things gladly, and with W. G. and E. M. both fielding close to the wicket, and neither having any too tender a regard for the batsman, perfect concentration of mind was difficult to attain. He appealed freely himself when he was bowling, and, subject to discipline, he approved of other members of his side appealing too. 'Why didn't you appeal, Fred?' he snapped at the bowler after the over. 'Well, sir,' said Roberts, 'I looked towards you at the time.' A young Gloucestershire amateur, not the bowler, once got a formidable Australian stonewaller given out, and there was some little unpleasantness. He asked W. G. if he had been right to appeal. 'Right,' was the answer; 'I should think you were right. Why, if you hadn't, we might never have got him out.' One small story on this point may be allowed, because it is so agreeably typical of all the parties concerned. F. S. Jackson, as it is still natural to call him, was playing for Yorkshire against Gloucestershire in his first season of county cricket. E. M. stood a minimum of yards away at point, W. G. almost equally near on the leg-side, and they 'chattered' across their victim in their best manner. Lord Hawke, the Yorkshire captain, made some excuse to come on the field, and said to the young batsman, 'Are these two old beggars trying to bustle you?' 'I don't know,' was the answer, 'but anyhow they can't.'

To W. G., cricket, being a game, was a vehicle for a practical, rough-and-tumble humour. Possibly he did not appreciate it so whole-heartedly when the joke was turned against himself, but that is an amiable weakness of practical jokers all the world over. He never let it seriously discompose him as E. M. sometimes did.

Once upon a time, so it is alleged, E. M. was batting to S. M. J. Woods, and was hit upon his, as ever, ungloved hand. He dropped his bat, and shook his fingers in pain, whereat somebody in the crowd guffawed, and made some audible remark. 'I can't stand that, Sammy,' he cried, and ran to the boundary. 'Who said that?' he asked the crowd. 'There he is, Doctor,' answered the crowd, indicating a youthful and now terrified delinquent trying to escape, whereupon the Coroner plunged in among the spectators in a pursuit which was, let us hope, unsuccessful.

Cricket with W. G. was never a game to be played in deathly silence. His voice was often to be heard on the field, in exhortation or comment. The sound of his, 'Keep your arm up, Fred,' to one of his bowlers, was familiar to the Gloucestershire side and its adversaries. Even E. M. did not escape criticism if it was thought that he ought to have got a catch.

The less serious the match, the greater licence of humour did W. G. allow himself. One of the most often demanded of Arthur Croome's stories related to some village match in which E. M. was bowling and W. G. fielding at point. There came a steady stream of appeals from E. M., all steadily refused. Then said W. G., confidentially, to the umpire, 'Never mind my brother, he's always appealing. Now when I appeal it *is* out.' An over or two passed, and then came, 'How's that?' from point, and out went the batsman. First-class umpires can neither be bustled nor bamboozled, but in any case W. G. would not have done that in a big match; the joke was suited to the occasion.

It is idle to deny, I suppose, that he led umpires rather a hard life; some of them may have been frightened of giving him out, but if he ever intimidated them it was certainly not of malice aforethought; it was rather that irrepressibly keen boy in him that had never quite grown up, and would break out now and then on the impulse of the moment. A boy naturally and properly thinks the umpire a beast who gives him out, and if there was a Peter Pan in the world it was Dr. W. G. Grace. On the whole it was fortunate for him that umpires are not a revengeful race; indeed they probably stood so much in awe of him as to give him sometimes the benefit of the doubt. I am afraid of retelling old stories, but here is one new at any rate to me. Gloucestershire were playing Essex, and, when he had made three or four, W. G. was, in the general estimation of both sides, caught and bowled by Mead. He stoutly declared it was a bump-ball, and, after some palaver, he went on batting. In due course, Kortright knocked his middle and leg

*Grace and beauty. The identity of W.G.'s companion is unknown.*

stumps down, and, as the Old Man made ready to depart, exclaimed, 'What, are you going? There's still one standing.' W. G. said he had never been so insulted in his life, 'but,' as the Gloucestershire narrator added, 'he'd made enough runs to win the match.'

More and more as time went on these little eccentricities were accepted, with a rueful and affectionate smile, as 'pretty Fanny's way.' Nevertheless a burning anxiety to enforce the law in one direction only must lead to disputes and more rarely to what is vulgarly known as a jolly row. Yet the rows passed: if W. G. did not always apologise, neither did he ever bear malice; he forgot, and others, as far as there was anything to forgive, forgave. Some men, we know, cannot look over the hedge; W. G. was so essentially lovable that he could steal a horse now and then. As at cricket so at golf he would employ, by way of a highly effective joke, certain devices not usually reckoned orthodox. It is recorded of him in a certain foursome competition that, finding one of his adversaries driving too far and too straight for his liking, he told him funny stories (despite the mild protests of his own partner) until all the drives ended in the gorse or the heather.

One of W. G.'s most engaging qualities, upon which all who knew him are agreed, was his unvarying kindness to young cricketers. He encouraged and advised them, sympathised with them in good or evil fortune, looked after them off the field, and saw that they did not feel lonely or shy. Save only when they gave themselves airs they were sure of a friendly and cheering word. When at his Jubilee dinner this trait of his was mentioned, W. G. said that he was afraid he had not always been so kind, and told the story of a luckless colt whom he had hit out of the ground four times running and so ended his career once and for all. But that was in the way of business, and then he could be, as was his bounden duty, the most ruthless of killers. Mr. Neville Cardus has told admirably the story, as told to him, of a young fast bowler who, on his first appearance for the Players, had the lash of the Doctor's bat laid on with so cruel a precision that when he went to bed at night he cried like a child. Yet, even in the heat of conflict, W. G. could do the kindliest and most generous things. Mr. George Brann when quite a young man had made 99 against Gloucestershire. W. G. approached H. V. Page, the bowler, and told him to give the young batsman any kind of ball that he wanted. The bowler asked how he would like it: Mr. Brann modestly expressed a preference for a long hop on the off, had it served up to him, and pulled it on to

*Grace's action*

his wicket. Virtue that time was more than its own reward, and so it was when he gave Abel, who had made 96, a slow full-pitch to leg, and saw the ball neatly deposited in the hands of square-leg, fielding deep on the boundary. It has been alleged in this case that having first promised the full pitch he then privily moved the fieldsman, but I do not believe it. The humour of such a proceeding would have appealed to him, but he would have resisted it.

W. G.'s kindness to the young consisted not so much in what he said as in what he made them feel. A good innings might earn no more than, 'Well played, youg 'un,' but the recipient of those words touched the stars with uplifted head. To one who had been summarily bowled, 'Rather you had that one than I,' brought balm beyond belief. Mr. Jessop has told me of his first match for Gloucestershire. He had been getting a great many wickets in second-class cricket and was reasonably complacent. He was put on first to bowl against Lancashire, against A. C. MacLaren and Albert Ward, and one of them was soon missed off him at the wicket. He bowled and bowled; he nearly bowled his heart out, and the reward of thirty-four overs or so was one wicket – l.b.w. He was feeling like a pricked bubble, utterly depressed, and then, when he got into the dressing-room, W. G. said to him, 'Well bowled,

young'un.' Instantly the air was full of trumpets, the whole world rosy and golden, and he thought that after all he might play for Gloucestershire again. He did tolerably well in another match or so, and W. G. said that he could give him a place in one of the two matches at Cheltenham – which would he like? Not unnaturally he chose the first, in the hopes that he might earn his place in the second, and there was never any more doubt.

W. G. did not as a rule try to teach his young men. This was natural enough in Mr. Jessop's case, for he saw that there was a natural genius, far more likely to be spoiled than improved; but, generally speaking, it was his practice to cheer, to sympathise but to let alone, leaving the young man to work out his own salvation. He was always particular in noting and praising good fielding, and, if the catch was off his own bowling, the praise was not the less hearty. Though he had himself profited by Uncle Pocock, he had no great belief in coaching, and thought too much of it could do a young cricketer great harm. He carried out this principle in playing with his own sons when they were children. His coaching did not go far beyond seizing the bat and saying, 'This is the way to do it.'

That he was worshipped by all the young amateurs who played under his banner is certain. There is a touching little story of Arthur Croome's, of how three young players on the Gloucestershire side, having, as they thought, been rather cavalierly treated, conspired to call W. G. 'Dr. Grace' for a short while, and how he worried himself and appealed to other people and plucked at his beard, wondering and wondering how he had hurt their feelings. Of course they relented, and were fonder of him than ever. Whether the professionals had quite the same feeling of adoration is doubtful. He could be a martinet, and treated them on occasions a little brusquely. While he was friendly, he had no notion of their being familiar with him. Perhaps, too, there was a slight, underlying tradition of hostility in the professional ranks, in that they thought he had made more money out of cricket than they had done and yet they were not amateurs. They all had naturally a vast respect for his powers, and many of them, such as Alfred Shaw, Shrewsbury, Abel and Murch, had a real affection for him as well. It was the 'family circle' of the Gloucestershire amateurs that had the warmest feeling of all, but it was difficult for even the most casual acquaintance not to be conscious of his lovableness and almost to dare to love him.

A more truly modest game-player than W. G. could not be

found. He knew how good he was, of course, but he never condescended or patronised, and never spoke of his own achievements. Occasionally, though not often, he would talk about old times, but then not of himself but of the cricketers of his youthful prime. Fred, always remembered with affectionate admiration, had done this or that, or George Freeman had been on the whole the finest fast bowler against whom he had ever played. 'He used to get you here,' he would say, pointing to the inside of his thigh; 'and the ball felt as if it was going on there, going round and round.'

W. G. was always fond of young creatures, whether they played cricket or not, and there are many stories of his friendliness to small boys and girls. I have myself a vivid memory of a day when he came in a car to call at my house in Chelsea on the way to a Walton Heath foursome. He saw my daughter, then aged about two, flattening a pudgy nose against the window, and kissed his hand to her with an air so pretty and gracious that I could never afterwards pass that street corner without recalling it. Similarly there is one story of W. G. and a boy, as to which I can almost persuade myself that I was present, though I most certainly was not. It was in one of his very last cricket matches for a team of illustrious veterans against Charterhouse. At luncheon there was introduced to him a boy, whose father had played for Gloucestershire. 'Very glad to make your acquaintance,' was his greeting, 'and I hope you're a better fielder than your father was. He was the worst that ever I did see.' Of all the W. G. stories that seems to me the pleasantest. He lives again in every word of it.

In writing a personal sketch of a famous man, it is usual to say something of his appearance. In the case of W. G. as a cricketer, this must be unnecessary. We all know the vast bulk, the black beard in later years streaked with grey, the red and yellow cap. There is, however, another aspect of him that is not familiar – W. G. as a private person in mufti, and not a flannelled general on the battlefield. One proud and lucky man possesses a photograph, which will remain unique, since the plate is broken. It shows W. G. in his everyday clothes just before he is going into the pavilion to change. It is the first morning of the deciding Test Match at the Oval in 1896; he has been looking at the wicket, and discussing with F. S. Jackson what is to be done if he wins the toss. On his head is one of those square felt hats which we generally associate with farmers. He wears a black tail-coat and waistcoat, built on easy-going lines with an expanse of watch-chain, dark

*W.G. with F. S. Jackson at the Oval, 1896.*

trousers, a little baggy at the knee, and boots made for muddy lanes. In one hand is a solid blackthorn stick with a silver band round it. Future generations who see that photograph will protest that this cannot be a mighty athlete about to lead the chosen of England to victory. It must be, they will say, a jovial middle-aged doctor discussing the price of oats with a patient or neighbour that he has met in the market-place. The man in that picture is W. G., but it is the one we do not know, the country doctor who had followed his father's business, and could never quite understand why no one of his three sons wanted to be a country doctor too.

The W. G. that we know best is not merely a celebrity but the central figure in a cricketing mythology. The stories about him are endless, and this can hardly be explained by the fact that he was the best of all cricketers, that he looked the part of a Colossus, and had an amusing way of saying characteristic things. There have been many other mighty players if admittedly below him; yet the sum of the stories about them all is, by comparison, negligible. Many of them, though very famous in their day, live for us now only as minor personages in the W. G. legend; they are remembered because they come incidentally into stories about him. In point of his personality, as it will be handed on by tradition for years to come, he towers as high above them as he towered above them in stature when he was alive. If this is not greatness, it is something for which it is hard to find another name. May we not say that, with all his limitations, his one-sidedness, his simplicity, W. G. possessed in an obscure and unconscious way some of the qualities of a great man?

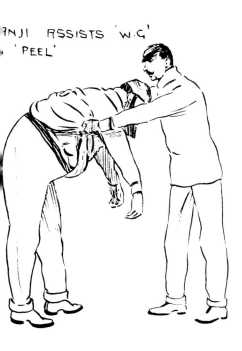

*After a match at Ranjitsinhji's home in Sussex in 1908, W.G. posed in Ranji's turban for this watercolour by H. S. Tuke.*

# 10

IT was characteristic of W. G. that he must always be doing something, preferably out of doors, and in the nature of a game or a sport. Cricket came first, but there were many other things to be enjoyed.

It has been mentioned that he was a good runner, but those who only saw him in middle life, when he lumbered down the pitch, found it hard to realise that in the lean and lanky days of his youth he had been a really fine athlete. It was when he was about eighteen that he entered, apparently on the spur of the moment, for a strangers' race at the Clifton College Sports, and won it. This inspired him to go on, and, from 1866 to 1870, he ran in a number of meetings not only in and around Bristol but at the London Athletic Club, the Crystal Palace, the Oval, Blackheath, and elsewhere, and won plenty of prizes. The most imposingly named race that he won was the quarter mile hurdle race of the National Olympian Sporting Association. This was the race, at the Crystal Palace in 1866, for which V. E. Walker let him off to compete in after he had made 224 for England against Surrey. Hurdle racing and sprinting were his strong points, and, of course, if a prize was given for throwing the cricket ball, it was his almost for the asking; his best throw was 117 yards. He also competed both in high and long jumps, but here his achievements were more modest. The

*Bristol Evening World* has published some of his best times, and, though they do not sound out of the ordinary today, it is to be remembered that they were mostly done on grass tracks, and probably not very good ones at that, since amateur athletics at the end of the 'sixties were in a primitive state. He is said to have done 100 yards on grass in $10\frac{4}{5}$ secs.; a quarter in $52\frac{1}{5}$; and 200 yards over hurdles in 28 secs. On one occasion, at the Long Ashton Sports, he won five events in an afternoon. This ability for foot-racing was shared by E. M., who is recorded to have beaten him in a 200 yards race, and descended to his two elder sons, both of whom were good runners. The younger W. G. won all manner of school races when a Clifton boy, though he did not attempt anything beyond the Freshmen's or College Sports at Cambridge.

In his quite young days, W. G. was fond of riding, but he did not go on with it for long, partly because he soon became a rather heavy burden for a horse, and partly because the sons in Dr. Grace's household had to make one horse do between them. He was a very good, as he was an enthusiastic, shot, and also extremely fond of fishing. There was a regular Graces' day of shooting every year at Badminton, and W. G. would shoot partridges at Scarborough before the festival cricket began, and get up early in the morning at Nottingham to catch barbel.

Regularly during the winter he ran with the Clifton Beagles, and

*Dr. Grace beagling*

later, when he left Gloucestershire, with the Worcester Park Beagles. Running gradually turned into jogging, and jogging almost into walking, but he covered an immense deal of ground, and was always there or thereabouts, while he was a good enough long jumper for any ditch that barred his way. He enjoyed the exercise, kept himself fit and kept his weight within bounds against the next summer.

When he went to the Crystal Palace he became an enthusiast for the game of bowls; he played a part in the founding of an international competition with Scotland, Ireland, and Wales; he captained England in the first match played at the Crystal Palace in 1903, and continued to do so till the Edinburgh match in 1908. He was also a keen curler, and his liking for the game, as well as his untiring enthusiasm for all games at all times, is illustrated by the record of one day of his life when he was sixty years old. He reached Maidenhead from his house at Mottingham before ten o'clock, to play in a golf match between cricketers and golfers. It rained hard all morning, and he played one round; it rained all the afternoon, and he played another; it cleared up after tea, and he played nine holes more. He took the train to London, curled all the evening at Prince's, and caught the last train home just after midnight.

He began to play golf when he was a few years over fifty, and continued to do so with increasing enthusiasm until the time of the war. Here I can say something from first-hand knowledge, as I had the great delight of playing in several foursomes with and against him at Walton Heath. He played golf with a mixture of keen seriousness and cheerful noisiness which was peculiar to him. It was never, as he played it, a silent game: there would come from him, periodically, immense shouts of laughter, or loud greetings to some friend playing another hole. And yet all the time he was trying as hard as he could, and trying to win. Occasionally, against particular opponents, he would entirely relax. Here, for instance, is the record, as given to me, of the early stages of the first hole at Rye as played by W. G. and W. L. Murdoch, after both had been in some trouble with the ditch.

W. L. M.: 'I've played five' (moderately true).

W. G.: 'Well, I've played two less than you.'

From a purely technical point of view, his golf, as I recollect it, was rather singular. He was an excellent putter, which was not in the least surprising, and no one ever extracted a greater poignancy of enjoyment from the holing of a long putt. There is still remembered a very long and curly one holed for a half at Walton

*W.G. at the Crystal Palace Bowling Club.*

*At a London bowling green in 1911, the Old Man wears a mourning arm-band for his brother, E. M. Grace.*

Heath, which caused him to lie down and roll on the ground in ecstasy. He drove very straight, standing firm-footed, with a short swing, and hitting the ball with little more than a flick of the wrist; but that flick was admirably timed, and his wrist work earned the high praise of no less a critic than James Braid. The one thing he could not do well was to play an iron shot. It is hard to understand why that extremely sound and simple method of his could not be applied to an iron club as well as a wooden one, but the irons beat him. When he had his driver in his hand, one perceived that here was a ball-hitting genius who had come to golf a little too late; with an iron he seemed a very ordinary mortal. There was a favourite nondescript iron of niblick ancestry which he called his 'cleaver,' and used in all possible situations, but it was not, in my recollection, very effective. It has always been said that good iron play is the hardest thing for a late beginner to learn, and I have always thought of W. G. as providing sound evidence of that truth.

He was not given to theorising about the game, but he tried as resolutely to put the club head against the ball as he had the bat: nor would any weather stop him once he had come to a course to play. To play with him was an exhilarating experience not to be forgotten.

Indoor games were not such fun as outdoor games, but they

*W.G.'s golfing instructor was G. W. Beldam, and in his own handwriting Grace writes on this photograph Beldam's comments on his golfing style.*

were a vast deal better than none at all, and W. G. was very fond of billiards, though not so good a player as would have been expected from the possessor of so supreme an eye for a ball. He did not play a great deal except on certain occasions, generally of a festal character. Every year, at Hastings, he played a match against the same opponent, which was one of the features of the festival, and every year he drove his enemy into a state of frantic but unavailing protest by potting him on every possible occasion. He was also very fond of whist, which he played well and with that feeling for the rigour of the game which belonged to his cricket. There were weekly whist parties at the house of one of his brothers-in-law, where it was as much as the life of any of the younger generation was worth to break the solemn stillness. I imagine that no Grace would have looked for any quarter after a revoke, and he certainly would not have given it.

*Caddies watch the great cricketer taking a short putt.*

# 11

THE Graces were essentially a clan, which absorbed its cousins – Pococks, Reeses, Gilberts, and the rest; absorbed its sons-in-law and daughters-in-law, and had for its chieftain Dr. Henry Mills Grace. When he died, Dr. Henry Grace the younger succeeded, as of right, and reigned undisputed. After his time, W. G. became the head of the family, and was loyally supported by his elder brother E. M.

They possessed this attribute of a clan, that they had a great admiration and affection for one another, and, though they might now and again squabble amongst themselves, they were always prepared to unite against any outsider. As in the case of Dr. Johnson and Garrick, no Grace would allow another to be abused except by himself. There is a story told of a certain match in which a catch went near E. M., who, apparently, made no vast effort to reach it. 'You ought to have caught it, Ted,' exclaimed W. G. 'It didn't come to me, Gilbert,' protested E. M. 'You ought to have caught it,' reiterated W. G., this time with such severity that another member of the Gloucestershire side was emboldened to say, 'Yes, Coroner, you ought to have caught it.' Thereupon the whole wrath of W. G. was turned upon the interloper, and the catch was forgotten. 'He was a Coroner,' said W. G. once of his brother, 'but I shouldn't like anyone to hold an inquest on his

*The Grace family on the occasion of their annual nutting-party.*

cricket.' And he probably meant exactly what he said; nobody but a Grace would have been allowed to do so.

This quality may have been the product of the Downend bringing up in a large and self-sufficient family. It was a busy household, in which there was only just time to dash in from a round of visits and fall instantly to cricket, and very little time to say 'please' or 'thank you.' Discipline was strict, criticism candid and unsparing, with no account taken of sensitive feelings. The elders said what they thought to the younger ones, and the younger ones took this as a natural state of affairs. But it was all inside the family circle. We remember what Henry said to the South Wales captain when he had asked the young W. G. to play, and then thought to leave him out of the side. To touch one of the Graces was to bring, in Dandy Dinmont's phrase, 'the whole clamjamfray,' down on the presumptuous offender's head.

That was one of their clannish characteristics, and another was that they had a liking for doing things in herds. There was a regular 'Graces' Day' of shooting at the Duke of Beaufort's, since there was an old connection between the big house at Badminton, and the small house at Downend. There used also to be, every summer, a tremendous nutting-party of Graces. Swollen by sisters, cousins, aunts, and grandchildren, it assumed formidable proportions, and swept over the country forty-five strong, as can be seen from a photograph of the group.

Not only were the Graces a clan, but they were a clan of countrymen, and never aspired to be anything else. Dr. Henry Mills Grace was a country doctor; he brought up all his sons to follow him. As one after the other they grew up and passed, sometimes in rather a leisurely manner, their medical examinations, the old patriarch took them and dotted them about the county in suitable practices – Henry at Kingswood Hill; E. M. at Thornbury; W. G. at Stapleton Road in Bristol; Alfred somewhere else, where perhaps, being the horsy one of the family, he could get a little hunting. No one of them essayed what might then have been called a 'genteel' practice. Rich patients were not for them. As their father had done before them, they drove far afield in their traps, and looked after poor people, whom they could understand and treat with homely kindness. That was their job: they were country doctors.

Theirs was a country home, with very little reading of books but much talk of horses and guns and all rustic things. W. G. had

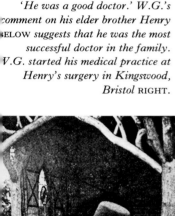

*'He was a good doctor.' W.G.'s comment on his elder brother Henry* BELOW *suggests that he was the most successful doctor in the family. W.G. started his medical practice at Henry's surgery in Kingswood, Bristol* RIGHT.

breathed into his growing frame the spirit of the country, and never lost it. He was fond of his garden, and had an instinct for it, so that it has been said of him that he 'could make anything grow.' He had such a 'way with him' with dogs, as he had with small children, that one dog, lent to him for a day's shooting, entirely declined to go back to its rightful owner, and had perforce to become a Grace by adoption for evermore. He knew birds and their ways and their songs, not through any conscious learning but because he was always the country boy that he had been born; and this sort of knowledge and this sort of nature were the common heritage of the family.

Much has necessarily been written of the sons of this remarkable family: nothing of the daughters. Their names at least ought to be recorded, if only because they fielded now and then in the Downend orchard. They were: Blanche, who married Mr. Dann, a local clergyman; Fanny, who did not marry; Alice, who married Dr. Bernard; and Annie, who married Dr. Skelton, her father's assistant. The doctoring tradition was thus well maintained, but the cricketing one apparently was not, for, though Mrs. Dann and Mrs. Bernard both had children, they produced no cricketers of note. Neither for that matter, except for the younger W. G.'s blue at Cambridge, has the cricketing strain descended through the sons. Genius flared high to heaven in one generation and then expired. Here is a problem over which the eugenists may ponder.

Now it is time to leave the family home at Downend and move on to the time when W. G. had a home and a family of his own. As early as the last years of the 'sixties he was beginning his studies at the Bristol Medical School, but no doubt cricket was a sad hindrance, and we have seen that it was not till near the end of the 'seventies that he blossomed into 'the Doctor'.

Meanwhile, on October 9th, 1873, he had married his cousin Miss Agnes Nicholls Day, whose father was in his day well known as a lithographer and had a large house on Clapham Common. Mrs. Grace is today remembered by many cricketers as a kindly and delightful hostess. It was destined to be a perfectly happy union, with an affection on both sides that remained fresh and youthful to the end. Four children were born to them; the late W. G. Grace Junr. in 1874, Edgar (later Vice-Admiral H. E. Grace, C.B.) in 1876, Bessy, who had the family genius for batting and died young, two years later, and, after several years interval, Charles, who could bowl lobs, dance down the pitch and paralyse bowlers by hitting sixes but scorned patience and defence.

For a little while the young couple lived in the west, and then moved to London, where W. G. went to Bart's. In 1876, when their second son was born, they lived in Earl's Court, and afterwards moved for a while to Acton. Then came the great day when W. G. had travelled through the night from Edinburgh to Lord's with his diploma in his bag, and Tom Emmett, slipping down on the wet grass, pointed to the green mark on his flannels, and said, 'No, sir, I'm not hurt, but I've got my diploma.'

It was time to settle down to a practice; one was found in Stapleton Road in Bristol, and here W. G. worked until he finally left Gloucestershire to take charge of the London County cricket at the Crystal Palace. I think it is too commonly believed that he did very little doctoring, and, indeed, that he was only a doctor by courtesy. If this is the general impression, it is wrong. W. G. was the official Parish Doctor in his district. All through the winter he worked hard at his profession, and had a practice large enough at any rate to warrant an assistant. In the summer of course, cricket did take up nearly all his time, and he had to have not one *locum tenens* but two. Even so he would look after his patients at the weekends, and, during a match in which he made two hundreds, he did not go to bed at all throughout one night but sat up with a poor woman whom he had promised to see through her confinement.

Stapleton Road was not what house agents would call a 'residential district,' and W. G. had not many well-to-do patients. One old lady left him a hundred pounds and some silver candlesticks, but she was the exception to prove the rule that his patients were poor people. Most of them would come to his surgery, and one of his small sons was discovered, to his mother's horror, with a nose flattened against an imperfectly frosted window, watching, spellbound, the amputation of a thumb. It was no doubt the kind of practice that best suited W. G., for he was fond of the people and could talk to them in their own language, and they in their turn were devoted to him.

Christmas was a great occasion, on which he and Mrs. Grace made a feast for their humbler neighbours. The institution grew and grew till in one year there was as many as a hundred guests. Everybody had to bring two pudding-basins. Into one was put roast beef and greens, and into the other plum-pudding. Over these two dishes, W. G. and his wife presided, while it was the children's business to hand out the oranges and apples. To one such festival there came an old lady of over ninety. W. G., hailing her as 'Granny,' asked how she had come, and said he would have

*W.G. with his wife at Ashley Grange*

sent to fetch her. 'Oh, it's all right, sir,' she replied. 'My gal brought me' – and the 'gal' was found to be another old lady of seventy-one. This was one of the unfading jokes, often told with glee, and never allowed to die.

When W. G. first began to practise in Stapleton Road, the family lived close by in a house called Thrissle Lodge, and afterwards moved to Thrissle House. Here there was a pitch in the garden, and before the season began in the spring the Gloucestershire eleven would come there for its early practice. It was not an ideal pitch, and ran slightly uphill, but it served its purpose. Later on again, there was a move to Clifton, first to a house in Victoria Square, and then, in order to be near the new county ground, to a pleasant house, more in the country, called Ashley Grange. The move to Clifton did not imply any lessening of work, for W. G. went regularly every day to his practice in Stapleton Road.

W. G. always made the most strenuous efforts to be home for Sunday (how he would have rebelled against the modern plan of starting a match on a Saturday!), and on the Sunday there was a regular family rite. Father and mother and children set out on a walk from Stapleton Road to see old Mrs. Grace at Downend. They came to a certain ridge where W. G. told how, as a boy, he had watched Lord Raglan's funeral procession from that very spot. On the ridge was waiting Granny in her pony carriage. She picked up her daughter-in-law and the baby of the moment and went forward, while the rest walked all the way. After tea the converse procedure was followed. The pony carriage went as far as the ridge and dropped its passengers, and the united family walked home together.

Besides the father and mother and the four children, the household had two permanent denizens in the shape of 'Uncle and Aunt Nicholls,' who came for a fortnight's visit, and settled down to live with the Graces for the rest of their lives. Uncle Pocock, now promoted to the rank of a great-uncle, was often to be found there, and was as kind to the younger generation as he had been to the nephews at Downend. He no longer coached at cricket but taught chess instead. One exciting thing about him was that he made a mysterious champagne of his own, for which he imported his own

*Ashley Grange*

*Henry Edgar, later Vice-Admiral,
Grace*

grapes. As to its quality, I have no precise knowledge; it must be left to the imagination. Dr. Henry Grace, now Uncle Henry, was also a great friend of the children. They were too young to know Fred, who had died in 1880, and could only remember with awe the sight of their father and mother getting into the carriage to go to the funeral. It was Fred, his one younger brother, that was closest to W. G.'s heart; he felt for him, perhaps, a sort of protective tenderness, and would often talk about him with admiring regret.

It was a very quiet household. At the time of cricket weeks at Clifton or Cheltenham there would be open house for cricketing friends, and there has often been quoted W. G.'s cheerful greeting to Mr. A. J. Webbe – 'It's all right, Webbie, its down the well' – in allusion to the champagne to be drunk at his house at dinner. These festivities were, however, exceptional, and, as a rule, life went on with very few dinner parties or amusements. There was not a great deal of money to spare, and the father and mother denied themselves for the sake of the children. Now and again they would go out for an evening – W. G. more magnificent than ever in an uncharted acreage of shirt-front – but this was an event. The Graces were a hardy family, and one small example may be given. The eldest son, Bert, was a day boy at Clifton College, and the second, Edgar, was going to a coach at Clifton in order to get into the Navy. The two boys walked every morning three and a half miles from Stapleton Road to Clifton, home for lunch, then back to work and home again at night. After a while this was deemed a little strenuous, and it was arranged for the boys to lunch at Clifton and so walk only seven miles a day instead of fourteen. Their father and uncles had thought nothing of walking several miles home after a match, carrying cricket-bags, and they were brought up in the same school.

This simple, frugal home life was the more marked because in those days in the west country to be a Grace was to be very much of a somebody. The Graces had, in the modern idiom, put Gloucestershire on the map, and it did not forget. Had they so desired it, W. G. and his wife could have been fêted to their hearts' content. As it was, something of royalty hedged them round. If W. G. were talking to a friend on the platform at Paddington, the train would wait respectfully for him to take his seat before it started westward, and great crowds would come to meet it at Bristol Station if it were bringing home a victorious eleven. Gloucestershire was the county of the Graces.

*The house at Mottingham*

W. G. would probably much have preferred to live in his native county all his days. The offer of the post of organising London County cricket was directly the cause of his leaving Gloucestershire, but that offer might never have been accepted had it not been for certain things which happened at Bristol having nothing to do with cricket. Details are unnecessary, but it may be said that a change in control and some rearrangement of districts caused several Parish Doctors to resign, and among them W. G. This left him comparatively high and dry as regards a medical practice, and so he felt inclined, and indeed almost bound, to accept the Crystal Palace offer.

The London County enterprise lasted from 1899 to 1905, and during that time W. G. lived near the Crystal Palace. When it ended he moved to a house in Mottingham, and remained there for the rest of his life. He was now sufficiently well-to-do; he could afford to retire. He had had heavy blows in the death of two of his children. His daughter Bessy, strikingly tall, handsome, and full of life, died of typhoid when she was in her very early twenties. His eldest son, Bert, who was a master at Osborne died of appendicitis in 1905. At Clifton he had a remarkable schoolboy career, being head of the school, captain of cricket and football, and a fine runner. Apart from his cricket already mentioned, he had done very well at Cambridge (he was at Pembroke), and had been a most popular and successful master at Osborne. His death perceptibly aged his father: for all his courage and natural high spirits, a little of W. G.'s youthful buoyancy was now gone for ever.

*W.G. in the conservatory at*
*Mottingham*

He had plenty of resources with which to fill up his time, for he had his games and his gardening, and apropos of the garden there is a story which exactly illustrates his liking for friendly little practical jokes. Mr. C. L. Townsend came to stay a night, and W. G. at once led him out into the garden, saying that on such an occasion they must have some asparagus for dinner. The asparagus beds were inspected, and were found rather disappointing. W. G. appeared a little depressed, but gathered a few heads of asparagus, said they must do the best they could, and led the way indoors. Dinner duly came, and with it the most resplendent dish of asparagus ever seen. The Old Man had carefully picked them before his guest's arrival and plotted his joke accordingly.

W. G.'s golf and bowls and curling, the amusements of the later years, are mentioned elsewhere, and there is not much to say about the noiseless tenor of his life at Mottingham. The war broke up his life, as it did everyone else's, and nobody took it more to heart. In addition to a father's anxieties, he had to bear the loss of so very

*W.G. in 1915, flanked by two soldiers. On the left, A. C. MacLaren. On the right, Ranjitsinhji.*

many young friends – not only the boys he knew but their fathers who had once been boys to him. He could not endure the thought of them being, as he said over and over again, 'mowed down.' His feelings induced him to do what was rare for him, namely write a letter to the newspapers, at the end of August 1914, protesting against any further public cricket, and urging all cricketers to set a good example in joining the Army.

In October of 1915 he was in his garden when he had a sudden stroke. He managed to get back to his house and was put to bed, and there he remained. The magnificent machine had run down at last, and his weakness was enhanced by the shock of an air raid in the neighbourhood. Probably the last of his cricketing friends to talk to him was Mr. Leveson-Gower, who was stationed near by and came over to see him. He said that the air raids worried him. 'You can't be frightened of aeroplanes, Old Man,' said his visitor. 'You, who had Jones bowling through your beard.' 'That was different,' he answered. 'I could see that Jones, and see what he was at. I can't see the aeroplanes.' He was obviously very ill, but he signed a photograph not only for Mr. Leveson-Gower's driver but for half a dozen other men in the battalion.

About a fortnight after he had been taken ill he tried to get out of bed, collapsed, and died at once. The funeral was on October 26th, 1915, and there were present many cricketers, a number of them in uniform, though only a small fraction of those who would have been there in other times. He lies buried in Elmer's End Cemetery by the side of his son and daughter.

*By the year Bernard Darwin was writing this biography of W. G. Grace, and the above photograph was taken, the MCC had already made their permanent tribute to the memory of the great cricketer : the Grace Gates at Lords.*

# STATISTICS

compiled by G. Neville Weston

*Runs and wickets in all classes of cricket*

| Year | First-class | | Minor Matches | |
| | Runs | Wickets | Runs | Wickets |
|---|---|---|---|---|
| 1857 | — | — | 4 | 0 |
| 1858 | — | — | 17 | 0 |
| 1859 | — | — | 12 | 0 |
| 1860 | — | — | 82 | 0 |
| 1861 | — | — | 102 | 3 |
| 1862 | — | — | 298 | 22 |
| 1863 | — | — | 673 | 70 |
| 1864 | — | — | 1,189 | 122 |
| 1865 | 197 | 20 | 1,972 | 175 |
| 1866 | 581 | 31 | 1,583 | 198 |
| 1867 | 154 | 39 | 654 | 71 |
| 1868 | 625 | 49 | 1,200 | 86 |
| 1869 | 1,320 | 73 | 1,026 | 81 |
| 1870 | 1,808 | 50 | 1,452 | 86 |
| 1871 | 2,739 | 79 | 1,074 | 106 |
| 1872 | 1,561 | 68 | 1,008 | 108 (Inc. Canada & USA) |
| 1873 | 2,139 | 106 | 925 | 123 |
| 1873/74 (Australia) | | | 866 | 66 |
| 1874 | 1,664 | 140 | 1,187 | 130 |
| 1875 | 1,498 | 191 | 1,293 | 217 |
| 1876 | 2,622 | 129 | 1,268 | 88 |
| 1877 | 1,474 | 179 | 997 | 211 |
| 1878 | 1,151 | 152 | 658 | 184 |
| 1879 | 993 | 113 | 35 | 19 |
| 1880 | 951 | 84 | 1,150 | 133 |
| 1881 | 917 | 57 | 1,360 | 172 |
| 1882 | 975 | 101 | 1,404 | 171 |
| 1883 | 1,352 | 94 | 1,096 | 100 |
| 1884 | 1,361 | 82 | 703 | 56 |
| 1885 | 1,688 | 117 | 494 | 57 |
| 1886 | 1,846 | 122 | 233 | 31 |
| 1887 | 2,062 | 97 | 409 | 45 |

| | | | | |
|---|---|---|---|---|
| 1888 | 1,886 | 93 | 138 | 33 |
| 1889 | 1,396 | 44 | 978 | 96 |
| 1890 | 1,476 | 61 | 218 | 20 |
| 1891 | 771 | 58 | 530 | 49 |
| 1891/2 | 448 | 5 | 555 | 50 (Australia) |
| 1892 | 1,055 | 31 | 53 | 17 |
| 1893 | 1,609 | 22 | 654 | 36 |
| 1894 | 1,293 | 29 | 613 | 77 |
| 1895 | 2,346 | 16 | 236 | 5 |
| 1896 | 2,135 | 52 | 261 | 14 |
| 1897 | 1,532 | 56 | 343 | 20 |
| 1898 | 1,513 | 36 | 272 | 13 |
| 1899 | 515 | 20 | 1,459 | 82 |
| 1900 | 1,277 | 32 | 1,398 | 130 |
| 1901 | 1,007 | 51 | 2,011 | 111 |
| 1902 | 1,187 | 46 | 1,458 | 115 |
| 1903 | 593 | 10 | 1,254 | 60 |
| 1904 | 637 | 21 | 944 | 111 |
| 1905 | 250 | 7 | 1,118 | 123 |
| 1906 | 241 | 13 | 876 | 68 |
| 1907 | 19 | — | 1,040 | 104 |
| 1908 | 40 | — | 684 | 116 |
| 1909 | — | — | 41 | 1 |
| 1910 | — | — | 418 | 21 |
| 1911 | — | — | 369 | 30 |
| 1912 | — | — | 139 | 3 |
| 1913 | — | — | 247 | 6 |
| 1914 | — | — | 205 | 4 |

W.G. made 871 catches in first-class matches and 641 in minor matches, a total of 1,512 catches. He also on occasions acted as wicket-keeper, and stumped 3 in first-class matches and 51 in minor matches, a total of 54.

### Grand Total of W.G.'s figures in all classes of cricket

| | Runs | Wickets | Catches | Stumpings |
|---|---|---|---|---|
| First-class matches: | 54,904 | 2,879 | 871 | 3 |
| Minor matches: | 44,936 | 4,446 | 641 | 51 |
| Grand Total: | 99,840 | 7,325 | 1,512 | 54 |

W. G. Grace scored 126 centuries in first-class matches and 95 in minor. *W. G. Grace Cricketer* by F. S. Ashley-Cooper (Wisden, 1916), generally to be accepted as a statistical record of his career, omits four of his centuries scored in minor matches. They are as follows:

> 1883, June 7 For Bristol Medicals v Lansdown.    150 not out (W.G. in this match also took 7 wickets and made 1 stumping)
> 1884, August 7 For East Somerset v Wells    117
> 1889, May 4 For J. H. Brain's XI v Cardiff    161
> 1901, July 4 For W. G. Grace Junior's XI v Oundle School    141

One century is incorrectly recorded by Ashley-Cooper, viz:

> 1866 (No month) For W. Absolon's XI v Eastern Counties Club    118.

This should have been:

> 1865, July 2 For Nicolson's United v Eastern Counties at Stratford, London    134

*    *    *    *    *

In first-class cricket he carried his bat through a completed innings on 17 occasions.

His highest first wicket partnership was of 283 with R. B. Cooper (101) for Gentlemen of South v Players of South at the Oval, 1869

For any wicket: 281 for the second with J. M. Cotterill (88) for South v North at Princes, 1877, and 281 for the third with L. Walker for London County v M.C.C. & Ground at the Crystal Palace, 1901.

He three times scored two separate hundreds in a match.

He five times made three separate hundreds in successive first-class matches.

He played a three figure innings and took ten or more wickets in a match on fourteen occasions.

He scored a thousand or more runs and took a hundred or more wickets in a season on eight occasions; in two of those seasons he scored over two thousand runs.

In first-class matches W. G. Grace was clean bowled twenty times by Alfred Shaw and fourteen times by Tom Richardson.

In minor matches he was clean bowled by his brother 'E.M.' six times, by his brother Fred twice and by his brother Henry, once.

In 1899 he was clean bowled by his son W. G. Grace junior.

*In 1868 W. G. Grace was playing for the United South of England XI against XXII of the Cadoxton Club at Knoll Park, Neath. A contemporary illustration of the match in progress is shown* ABOVE. *W.G. was twice dismissed by G. Howitt for a duck. The bat with which he failed to score is still treasured in a glass case at Neath.*

He was never twice dismissed for 0 in a first-class match.

W.G. made every score from 0 to 100 in first-class matches, and in minor matches every such score except 98.

In first-class matches he made his first duck on June 22 and 23, 1865, for Gentlemen of the South v Players of the South at the Oval; and completed his 0–100 sequence in 1898 in such matches by making 93 in August, 3, 4 and 5, for Gloucestershire v Sussex, at Bristol. His first duck in minor matches was made on August 10 and 11, 1857, for West Gloucs. v Clifton on Durdham Down and his last score in this sequence was 79 scored for Eltham against Bickley Park, at Eltham on June 24 1911.

On May 23, 24 and 25, 1895, W.G., at the age of 47, was on the field during every ball of the match. He made 257 and 73 not out, and took two wickets (in 215 balls).

On June 1 1907, W.G. played for both sides in a match between London County and Worcester Park Beagles, at the Crystal Palace. This was an annual match between these two teams. For the County he made 25 runs and for the Beagles he made 1 catch. The latter lost five wickets in making 49 runs in reply to the County's total of 153.

# BIBLIOGRAPHY

compiled by G. Neville Weston

Alpha of the Plough, *Pebbles on the Shore*. London 1917

Altham, H. S., *A History of Cricket*. London 1926

Arlott, J., *Concerning Cricket*. London 1949

Ashley-Cooper, F. S., *Edward Mills Grace – Cricketer*. London 1916
— *Cricket Scores and Biographies*, Fifteen Vols. 1862–95
— *W. G. Grace – Cricketer*. London 1916

Beldam, G. W. and C. B. Fry, *Great Batsmen – their methods at a glance*. London 1905

Bradfield, D., *The Lansdown Story*. Bath 1971

Brownlee, W. M., *W. G. Grace – a biography*. London 1887

Cardus, N., *A Cricketer's Book*. London 1922
— *Cricket*. London 1930

Daft, R., *A Cricketer's Yarns*. London 1926
— *Kings of Cricket*. Bristol 1893

Dewar, W., Ed., *The Cricket Annual*. 1892

Fry, C. B., *Life Worth Living*. London 1939

Fitzgerald, R. A., *Wickets in the West*. London 1873

Furniss, H., 'A Century of Grace' in *How's That?* Bristol

Grace, W. G., *Cricket*. Bristol 1891
— *The History of a Hundred Centuries*. London 1895
— and W. Stonehewer, *The Bowler's Annual for 1907*. London
— *W.G.* London 1899
— *W.G.'s Little Book*. London 1909

Hawke, Lord, Lord Harris and Sir Home Gordon, Eds., *Memorial Biography of Dr W. G. Grace*. London 1919

Iliffe & Sons, *The Hero of Cricket*. London. N.D.

Massingham, H. and H. J. Massingham, Eds, *The Great Victorians*. London 1932

Pentelow, J. N., 'The Noblest Roman of them All', in *Ayres' Cricket Companion*, 1916.

Powell, A. G., and S. Canynge Caple, *The Graces*. London 1948 and 1974.

Sewell, E. H. D., *An Outdoor Wallah*. London 1945
— *Cricket under Fire*. London 1941
— *The Log of a Sportsman*. London 1923

Steel, A. G. and R. H. Lyttleton, *Cricket*. London 1888 and c.

Tate, H. A., *Life, Scores and Mode of Dismissal of 'W.G.' in First-Class Cricket*. London 1896 and 1897

*Bibliography*

Thomson, A. A., *The Great Cricketer*. London 1957 and 1968

Waring, A. J., *'W.G.', or The Champion's Career*. London 1896

Warne, F. G., *Dr W. G. Grace – the king of cricket*. Bristol 1899

Weston, G. N., *W. G. Grace – the great cricketer*. Liskeard 1973

*Wisden*, 1864 to date (especially 1896 and 1916)

Wye, A., *Dr W. G. Grace*. London 1901


*Periodicals containing articles on W. G. Grace and his family*

*Cricket* 1882–1914

*The Cricket Field* 1892–95

*The Cricketer* 1921 to date

*Baily's Magazine of Sports and Pastimes* 1860–1926, particularly volumes 7, 19, 34 and 63.

## Picture Credits

The publisher would like to thank the following for permission to reproduce illustrations: University Library of the University of Bristol: 39 below; Marylebone Cricket Club: 27, 35, 57, 59 top, 62, 63, 73, 95, 98 below, 102 right, 119 top; Mary Evans Picture Library: 16, 17, 22, 23, 25, 32, 41, 46, 58, 61 left, 74; Radio Times Hulton Picture Library: 43, 51, 65, 87, 108 below, 120; Reece Winstone: 18, 56, 111 right, 115. The remaining illustrations come from the G. Neville Weston Collection, including the Harry Furniss cartoons of W. G. Grace which open each chapter.

# INDEX